D0218714

#RUN YOUR RACE

Crystal Krachunis

Copyright © 2017 Crystal Krachunis
Scripture quotations taken from the Amplified® Bible (AMP),

Copyright © 2015 by The Lockman Foundation
Used by permission. www.Lockman.org

Scripture taken from the New King James Version®.
Copyright © 1982 by Thomas Nelson, Inc.
Used by permission. All rights reserved.
Hatfield, Heather. "Runner's High: Is it Real?" WebMD.
3 March 2016. <http://www.webmd.com/fitness-
exercise/features/runners-high-is-it-for-real#1
Chambers, Oswald. My Utmost For His Highest. updated version.
Oswald Chambers Publications Association, LTD. 1992

S P H

SEAWARD
PUBLISHING HOUSE

Seaward Publishing House
17255 139th Pl. SE
Renton, WA 98058

Editorial work done by: Lisa Cerasoli at www.529books.com
ISBN 978-0-9995173-0-7

Acknowledgments

I would like to thank my husband and best friend, Matt. I would not be the person I am today without your constant love, support, and encouragement. Thank you for choosing me and walking beside me in this life, for better and for worse. You are my biggest fan. We are like peas and carrots. I love you, baby!

A special thanks to Pastor Connie Ong. Thank you for your assistance and prodding encouragement to just get it done! I love you and appreciate your wisdom. Thank you for believing in me.

Thank you, Mom and Papa, for your prayers. I know I would not be here today without them, or you! I love y'all.

Contents

"Therefore we also, since we are surrounded by so great a cloud of witnesses, let us lay aside every weight, and the sin which so easily ensnares us, and let us run with endurance the race that is set before us, 2 looking unto Jesus, the author and finisher of our faith, who for the joy that was set before Him endured the cross, despising the shame, and has sat down at the right hand of the throne of God"

Hebrews 12:1-2

Introduction

"I was born a poor black child." Oh wait, that's not my story—that's Steve Martin's story in *The Jerk*, and one of my favorite movie lines that I like to quote often. My story is a little different. I share a portion of my story in this book, which has taken me five years to complete. Why so long? I started out writing a "Daily Word" for the ladies in my church, because I would gain insight into a lot of "spiritual disciplines" while I was running. So, I'd jot down those thoughts in an email, sending out one a day, just about different things, always trying to use my life experiences as examples. I worked to be transparent in these notes in the hopes that people could relate. I shared my triumphs and my struggles through my Christian walk so that others may learn what works well and what doesn't without having to make all the mistakes I have. My pastor in Texas always told us, "Don't reinvent the wheel. Take what others have done and use it going forward." As I was running along one day, I got the idea that these "Daily Words" might be nice in book form. I conceived of a book with thirty-one chapters, one for every day of the month. People could read one a day and start over, or read the whole book at once, whatever they preferred—kind of like a "Proverbs for the Running Christian." Once I got that idea, I found myself writing a little, then putting the book down for months at a time, when the devil would hit me with negative thoughts of unworthiness. *Nobody cares about you or this book. It's a dumb idea. You are dumb. Nobody cares. Nobody will read it.* So, I would stop and get back to busying myself in the ministry and lose all thoughts of this book idea. I finally shared my concept with a good friend, Pastor Connie, about a year ago and she encouraged me to finish writing. She said, "Do the work, finish your book, and God will take care of everything else."

So, here I am, five years later, presenting *Run Your Race* to you.

I rely heavily on the Word of God in my life. I love His Word and so this book is chock-full of scripture. His Word is life and health to our flesh and souls. I hope you hear my heart in this book and I pray that you grow in your relationship to God and in spiritual maturity. And I hope you learn to run hard and to love the race set before you!

Chapter 1

A Runner Runs

Do you like to run? There's a loaded question. Don't worry, there's no judgment if you hate running. I imagine most people might say, "No! Why would you ask such a stupid question?" I think if most people chose any exercise, it would not be running. Maybe walking? Hiking? Biking? But, hey, I like to run. I'm a forty-something female, and I run on average twenty miles a week. I'm not a professional, but I consider myself a runner.

In March of 1995, I moved from Charlotte, NC back to my hometown of San Antonio, TX in order to take care of my grandmother, Elaine. I heard a salvation message and knew God was calling me to leave my current situation. I met God at the altar of a small church in San Antonio on a humid Wednesday night. It was during this time of my life that I began running seriously.

Grandma had severe rheumatoid arthritis and was confined to a wheelchair. Her hands and knees were frozen; the RA had severed the tendons connecting them to her limbs. I had to feed her, shower her, take her to the bathroom, and clean up after her. I was her chauffeur and maid. It was quite a handful for a newly-saved twenty-three-year-old that had a mountain of problems, bad habits, and sins to overcome.

So, I began running in order to relieve my stress. Every night after feeding my grandma and putting on her favorite television program, I took to the pavement. I would run until I couldn't run anymore. I would run and pray. Back in those days, I swear I ran fifty miles a week.

I learned a lot during that period of my life; how to be patient, kind, forgiving; how to control my anger and frustration; how to serve whole-heartedly; how to serve and not expect anything in return. Hard, but important and crucial lessons. Yet, I allowed God to teach me, mold me, shape me for His purpose and benefit. I wanted everything I was to be gone, and I wanted to become everything He wanted me to be.

I now live in Seattle, WA. It rains about 80 percent of the year, which means if you're like me and like to run outdoors, you're running in the rain. There's nothing like it—I swear I can smell the color green when I run, and it's amazing—but I digress. I love the feel of the rain on my face.

As I was preparing to go on my run this morning, and attempting to force my husband to run with me, he said, "But it's raining outside."

"Yes, it is," I replied, "But a runner runs no matter what the weather."

And that's when it hit me: a runner runs no matter what. Ask any runner, and they'll tell you there's no other exercise like running. There is no other "high" like a runner's high, and if you miss a day of running, you get the "blues." Running is addictive. I think in the last twenty years, the longest span I've gone without running was the six weeks I had to wait after my kids were born, and I wasn't very good at the waiting part. (Yes, I ran while I was pregnant, right up until the day before I gave birth to my son. Be sure to check with your doctor before attempting any form of exercise while you are pregnant.)

Every morning I wake up at 6:00 a.m. and prepare to run. I put on my exercise clothes, eat a protein bar for energy, and have a cup of coffee. Then I drop my daughter, Faith, off at her bus stop, and go for a run. I set boundaries around this time and I am always diligent to follow through. I run in any kind of weather, and I even run when I'm sick. "Oh my," you say? Don't worry, I've researched this. As long as your symptoms are above the neck with no fever, it's okay. I don't let anything stop me from running. We go on vacation, I run. A runner runs.

> "Therefore we also, since we are surrounded by so great a cloud of witnesses, let us lay aside every weight, and the sin which so easily ensnares us, and let us run with endurance the race that is set before us" **Hebrews 12:1. NKJV**

Watching the world every morning, seeing the beauty God has created, looking at the giant trees that Seattle is so famous for—it puts my life in perspective. It enables me to feel oneness with God. I bring that home along with my runner's high and I share that with my family. I want that for you. I literally run to God every morning to recharge. Running clears my head and helps prepare me for my day. It is part of my quiet time with the Lord, where my ears and heart are open to His words and ways and my spirit willingly receives them. While I listen to the rhythm of my cadence, I can hear His heart beat and I am in sync with Him. This is a "high" that you cannot tell someone about, or even begin to describe, but can only experience in the presence of the Most High. However, you don't have to love running to do what I do, to find and be one with the Holy Spirit. I wrote this book to express my love for God, and I'm using running as an analogy for that because I believe in my heart the running part has become a bridge for me. I hope this book will help you find your bridge. I pray that you will use these disciplines within to run faster and harder toward God's will and purpose for your life. I pray that you know your value and the height and depth of His love, His crazy jealous love for you!

If you are anything like me, you struggle with your value. I sought my value for years in other things—in people, personal possessions, various jobs, but mostly with grades. I was always an intelligent kid. I graduated high school with a 3.98 and carried a 4.0 through most of college. I prided myself on getting good grades. It was where I found my value. I wasn't raised in a "normal home"; I never knew my father. Not only did I not know him, I had never even seen a picture of him growing up. My mother was a horrible alcoholic who sought value in obtaining her next high from her current boyfriend. I grew up in a home where I was never encouraged, loved, or valued. I existed. Until I met Him.

According to Scripture, before Jesus, you were described by your sin. Sin defined you. It held you in bondage. But when He came into your life, He set you free and drew you to His arms. In much of the Christian world, you hear how "unworthy" you are. But, I'm here to tell you how valuable you are. The lie the world tells you is that you determine your own value. Well, I'm here to tell you He determines your value. His word declares it!

> "Fear not, then; you are of more value than many
> sparrows" Matthew 10:31. **NKJV**

Your sin did separate you. But when you received Him, when you were born again of His Spirit, you became His child. You are valuable to Him, even while you were in your sin.

Almighty God left all His glory and robed Himself in flesh to come to earth to die for you, and that makes you *valuable*. He looked past your sin and saw value in you. I think that makes you worth-full. How much more after you become His are you valuable to Him? This is the gospel in a nut shell:

> "For our sake He made Christ [virtually] to be sin Who knew no sin, so that in *and* through Him we might become [endued with, viewed as being in, and examples of] the righteousness of God [what we ought to be, approved and acceptable and in right relationship with Him, by His goodness]"
> **2 Corinthians 5:21. AMP**

You are of much value to Him. Not what you do, but who you are in Him. There is a confidence that comes from knowing who you are in Christ. Notice I said confidence and not cockiness. It is a confidence that is in Him alone, never in yourself or your ability, or lack thereof.

This confidence doesn't happen overnight. It takes time, lots and lots of time, being in His presence, seeking His face, communing with Him, getting to know Him intimately. It takes time for Him heal you, restore you, deliver you, and ultimately fill you up! Be patient with yourself. Pray and wait on Him. He is worthy and you are worth it.

I wear a size-12 running shoe. That's a big foot! Yeah, I get it. I hated having big feet as a kid. When all the other little girls around me had petite feet, I had clown feet. I was always subconscious of how big my feet were. I would even try to squeeze my big feet into smaller shoes so they'd appear smaller, but I only ended up getting horrible ingrown toenails.

My mom had a friend that took pity on me for having such large feet. She bought me a Cinderella book from a local author, except this Cinderella had big feet. They were so big that both of her evil step sister's feet—yes, all four feet—could fit into one glass slipper. It was like the size of a punch bowl! Now, that's my kind of Cinderella. I wish I still had that book; it made me feel good about my big feet. In order to run your race, you're going to have to be okay with your flaws and imperfections, with your "big feet." You are going to have to learn to love yourself the way God made you. I didn't love myself. I grew up in New Mexico and San Antonio. My best friends growing up were Hispanic. I loved everything about the Mexican culture. I loved my friend's skin color and I hated my white skin. I loved her black curly hair and dark eyes. I loved her family. I loved her mom and dad and her grandma and grandpa. (Her grandpa used to let me call him "Pappo.") I loved Mexican food and I still do. I love tacos, enchiladas, burritos, carne asadas, guacamole, and I could go on and on. But, I grew up wanting to be and look like someone else.

I was made fun of for being white and was called names. I had one girl always trying to fight me just because of it. I hated my skin. As an adult Christian, I can look back and see that what I wanted was the family and stability that my friend had and that I saw in the Mexican culture around me. I didn't necessarily want to look Mexican, I wanted a family that loved each other, spent time together, went on vacations, sat down for dinner—all the things that I was lacking in my life.

The Lord has taken His time in healing the identity crisis I had struggled with since my childhood. It has taken many years for me to get to a place where I love myself with all my "flaws" and imperfections, a place where I am okay just knowing that I am His and "loving the skin I am in." I am beloved in His sight.

Here are two scriptures that have helped me with accepting my identity:

> "I will praise You, for I am fearfully and wonderfully made; Marvelous are Your works, And that my soul knows very well" **Psalm 139:14. NKJV**

> "When my father and my mother forsake me, Then the Lord will take care of me" **Psalm 27:10. NKJV**

To run your race, you have to know who you are and who you are running for. You have to know that He made you with those size-12 feet because you would fall over if they were any smaller. He made you with that beautiful skin color because He liked you in it. He thought you would be your most beautiful and do your best work in that color.

He is not the gingerbread man, cutting out cookie dough with His cookie cutter, where everyone is the same and everyone gets the same three candy buttons. He wonderfully and awesomely made you. He takes care of you better than a mother. He is an amazing Father. However, you have to know these things for yourself. Get in the Word and find out what He says about you. You are going to have to do a little pulling of the weeds in order to run this race. Pull out those lying and deceiving weeds that maybe you've sown or others have sown into your heart, and start planting the good seeds of God's Word.

This race isn't always easy and if you wear shoes too small, you'll develop ingrown toenails and you'll stop running—and a runner by definition, runs. God has set before you *your* race. It looks different than my race. Will you run the race set before you?

Chapter 2

You Cannot Fake Being a Runner

It happens every January 1: New Year's Resolutions. The gym is full of people making exercise commitments for the new year. Perhaps you've made some this year that you did or didn't keep, or are thinking about new ones that you may or may not keep for the next year. In any case come the first of January the treadmills at the gyms are packed and the roads and trails are full of runners that have started their resolutions.

These "runners" go out and buy themselves the right shoes, the right clothes, a Nike headband that proclaims Just Do It®, and possibly some new head phones to look cool while running. They even tell their friends, "I'm a runner." These "runners" have all but disappeared from the treadmills and the road by about mid-February. They'll show up periodically after that, making the excuse, "I've just gotten so busy." But, for the month of January, they looked like runners. (*I'm not knocking folks that aren't natural runners, or people that can't seem to make their New Year's resolution to "go to the gym" stick. There's a big picture here, so please stay with me.)

It doesn't matter if you dress the part and get out there a few times, a runner runs—it is the defining characteristic of the runner. We run and we run often. Running is a huge part of a runner's life. In fact, the definition of runner is "one who runs"– not part time, not sometimes, but all the time.

If I told you I was a flutist you would think, *She plays the flute.* Well, I played the flute many, many years ago. I do not currently play the flute. I don't practice it. My daughter is currently a flutist. She plays and practices every day. I picked hers up the other day and was able to play "All Out of Love" by Air Supply and I totally shocked myself with my ability to remember the notes and keys. Be that as it may, I am not a flutist.

My dog even recognizes a runner. Ranger knows by the clothes I put on if I am going for a run or not. As soon as I get up in the morning, he gets up and follows me around. I go to the kitchen, he goes to the kitchen. I go downstairs, he goes downstairs. He is following me waiting to see what clothes I'm going to wear. After I get the kids out the door, he follows me into the bedroom and sits at the foot of my bed to see what I'm going to do. He's a funny dog. He watches me and if I get in the shower, he'll go back into the living room and stare longingly out the bay window. But, if I get out my running pants and shirt, and he sees me put on my headband, it's go time! Observant dog.

Jesus knows who His runners are. A Christian is "one who lives in Christ." Just as a Texan lives in Texas, so a Christian lives in Christ. I know a lot of people who go to church, give to the poor, feed the homeless, take care of others, but they are not in Christ. Lots of people are loving and kind, but they are not in Christ. It's not what you do that makes you a Christian, it is only in Christ that you are a Christian.

Jesus said we need a new nature. We were born with a sinful nature and therefore, the Bible says we need a new nature:

> "Jesus answered him, I assure you, most solemnly
> I tell you, that unless a person is born again
> (anew, from above), he cannot ever see (know, be
> acquainted with, and experience) the kingdom of
> God. Nicodemus said to Him, How can a man be born
> when he is old? Can he enter his mother's womb
> again and be born? Jesus answered, I assure you,
> most solemnly I tell you, unless a man is born of
> water and [even] the Spirit, he cannot [ever] enter
> the kingdom of God" **John 3:3-5. AMP**

Jesus says you must be born again. Born of His spirit and having His spirit is what makes you His. It is the token that you belong to Him.

I wear a wedding band as a token that I am married to my husband. I said my vows to him and we made a covenant before God, and now I wear a ring as a token to my covenant with Matt. The Holy Spirit is the token or seal to which you are in covenant with God. Notice these scriptures (Emphasis mine):

> "In Him you also who have heard the Word of Truth,
> the glad tidings (Gospel) of your salvation, and have
> believed in *and* adhered to *and* relied on Him, were
> stamped with the seal of the long-promised Holy
> Spirit" **Ephesians 1:13. AMP**

> "And do not grieve the Holy Spirit of God [do not
> offend or vex or sadden Him], by Whom you were
> sealed (marked, branded as God's own, secured) for
> the day of redemption (of final deliverance through
> Christ from evil and the consequences of sin)"
> **Ephesians 4:30. AMP**

Because of His nature, you cannot fake having the Holy Spirit. The work of the Holy Spirit in your life will be evident. He brings a change of nature from our old sinful life to a new life in Christ. Instead of living a life marred by sin, you now live life marked by righteousness. It will be evident to everyone around you. People who are in Christ even look different. They smile more and look less "hard" because there is a softening that takes place, even in their physical appearance.

Those in Christ, can spot a fake. There are people out there that can speak good *Christianese*, but a true God follower can discern those who have the Spirit and those who are fake. Just like my dog spots the runner, Jesus spots the fake:

> "Not everyone who says to Me, Lord, Lord, will enter the kingdom of heaven, but he who does the will of My Father Who is in heaven. Many will say to Me on that day, Lord, Lord, have we not prophesied in Your name and driven out demons in Your name and done many mighty works in Your name? And then I will say to them openly (publicly), I never knew you; depart from Me, you who act wickedly [disregarding My commands]" **Matthew 7:21-23. AMP**

On that day, Jesus says, "I never knew you." This is personal. He wants to know you intimately. He's not satisfied with good works. Your good works will not save you. He wants to live in you and have you live in Him. The key words in this are: "You who act wickedly." In the KJV, it reads: "Ye that work iniquity." These fake runners proclaimed they knew Jesus, but they never had a nature change. They continued to live a life of sin, i.e. iniquity. They were never endowed with the new nature of the Holy Spirit. The fake "runner" lives a life in the flesh.

Yikes!

"But you are not living the life of the flesh, you are living the life of the Spirit, if the [Holy] Spirit of God [really] dwells within you [directs and controls you]. But if anyone does not possess the [Holy] Spirit of Christ, he is none of His [he does not belong to Christ, is not truly a child of God]" **Romans 8:9. AMP**

God wants to live in you. He preordained it before the foundation of the world. He's always wanted to live in your presence. He longs for you. He longs to know you.

The mark of the Holy Spirit is a mark of righteousness. His nature is a nature of righteousness. You may not be sinless; you just begin to sin less. You no longer live a life according to that sinful nature, ruled and dictated by its lusts and desires, but are ruled by the promptings and urgings of the Spirit of righteousness according to the Bible:

"Boys (lads), let no one deceive *and* lead you astray. He who practices righteousness [who is upright, conforming to the divine will in purpose, thought, and action, living a consistently conscientious life] is righteous, even as He is righteous. By this it is made clear who take their nature from God *and* are His children and who take their nature from the devil *and* are his children: no one who does not practice righteousness [who does not conform to God's will in purpose, thought, and action] is of God; neither is anyone who does not love his brother (his fellow believer in Christ)" **1 John 3:7, 10. AMP**

Righteousness. It's the mark of the Holy Spirit. It is the mark of Jesus. Read what the psalmist prophesied concerning the Lord:

> "Your throne, O God, is forever and ever; the scepter
> of righteousness is the scepter of Your kingdom"
> **Psalm 45:6.**

A scepter is a symbol of sovereignty. Beautiful, sweet, amazing righteousness. It means you take on His nature of righteousness. He has exchanged His robe of righteousness for your filthy rags. You see how He sees. You love what He loves. You hate what He hates. This is where the phrase "Love the sinner, but hate the sin" comes from. You love what He loves–the sinner. You hate what He hates–the sin. You begin to love and serve righteousness and hate iniquity.

If you are in Christ, you are righteous before Him! Do not allow the world to tell you who you are, let Him. Do not allow the world to tell you how to act, let Him!

> "And having been set free from sin, you have become
> the servants of righteousness (of conformity to the
> divine will in thought, purpose, and action)"
> **Romans 6:18. NKVJ**

My husband and I came from different sides of the track. He was saved at the young age of fifteen and I didn't receive Christ until I was twenty-three and I had lived the wild life. There's not a sin out there that I didn't participate in. I lived life to the fullest of sinful ways.

My husband and I met and went on a few group dates. He attended my church on Sunday mornings and Wednesday nights. We saw a couple of movies together and had a few cups of coffee. Then I had a dream. After about three weeks of "dating," the Lord gave me a dream. In this dream, Matt and I were building a church, brick by brick. As a brick mason would, we slathered on the cement and layered each brick over and over again. I woke up and wondered what this meant.

Matt came to see me that night after I got off work. I shared the dream with him. He began to weep.

"I'm called into the ministry," he said. "And I only joined the Army to run away from God and my calling."

So, we cried and prayed as to what this meant for the two of us together. Matt struggled with marrying me because of my past. To put it bluntly, I was not a virgin and he was. He had saved himself for his wife. And me, well, I was taught the '70s hippy way: "*Make love, not war.*" I was never directed and guided in God's path, so I did what the world said I should do—experience sex. Matt wanted God's will, but he thought God's will would lead him to a woman who was like him—to a cute youth group girl that was a virgin. God's ways are not our ways. Praise Jesus! Matt began praying about me and he received clear words from the Lord: "*What I have cleansed, you do not call unclean.*" Righteousness came running! Matt never struggled with my past again.

You have a past, let it go. Let the past be the past. You are now clean! You are now righteous in Christ! Do not listen to the lies of the devil. It doesn't matter how you feel, it only matters what he says about you!

Chapter 3

Eat Healthy

What you eat determines how well you perform in day-to-day activities. If you eat too much sugar, consequently, you will never have enough energy. You will have "high highs" and "low lows." If you drink too much caffeine, you will get a morning jolt, but with an afternoon lull, usually followed by a nap or another jolt of coffee. It's a vicious cycle.

I read a lot about diet specifically as it relates to running. I have tried different "eating plans," but I always fall back on just eating a well-balanced, nutritionally sound diet.

On nights where I eat a well-balanced meal with protein and carbohydrates, I find that I can run farther and faster than, say, when nights when I eat a salad, but then indulge in cookies. My morning runs after eating a nutritionally-lacking meal are slow, sluggish, and I down-right fight to get through them. Food matters if you're going to be a runner.

Most marathon runners will eat a high carbohydrate meal the night before their race. This enables them to pull energy from reserves in the body, maintain a good pace, and finish strong.

Such as it is in our spiritual lives. What we feed our spirit matters. Every morning while I am having my morning coffee, I read my Bible and pray. I don't go a day without doing these two things. Praying and reading my Bible. Every. Single. Day. No matter what. I guard this time and set boundaries around this time. It's important.

When we are born again of God's Spirit, we have a new heart. We have died with Christ and become a new creation; but we still need to renew our minds. We have to constantly and consistently cast out old thoughts and ways, and replace them with God's thoughts and God's ways. How do we know His thoughts and His ways? BY HIS WORD. His Word is fuel for the soul. As a well-balanced meal provides all the nutrients for the body to operate effectively, so God's Word gives us spiritual vitality. It's the only truth and it brings wisdom.

The world wants us to act and think like it does, but the world is contrary to God. If we feed on the wisdom of the world, when we run, we will not be able to finish.

I never walk on my runs. In my mind, I have failed if I have to walk. A runner runs, she doesn't walk.

> "Yet when we are among the full-grown (spiritually mature Christians who are ripe in understanding), we do impart a [higher] wisdom (the knowledge of the divine plan previously hidden); but it is indeed not a wisdom of this present age *or* of this world nor of the leaders *and* rulers of this age, who are being brought to nothing *and* are doomed to pass away" 1 Corinthians 2:6. AMP

> "For this world's wisdom is foolishness (absurdity and stupidity) with God, for it is written, He lays hold of the wise in their [own] craftiness" 1 Corinthians 3:19. AMP

In order to run this race set before us, we must have God's wisdom. Feed on God's Word! It's the only food that sustains. It's the only food that you will be able to endure to the end. It's the only food that will enable you to run without quitting. God will supply the grace and mercy, but it's up to you to read and devour His Word. God will not force you to study His Word. He prompts and nudges; but in the end, it's completely up to you to decide what food you put in your body.

> "Do you not know that in a race all the runners compete, but [only] one receives the prize? So run [your race] that you may lay hold [of the prize] *and* make it yours" **1 Corinthians 9:24. AMP**

> "Holding out [to it] *and* offering [to all men] the Word of Life, so that in the day of Christ I may have something of which exultantly to rejoice *and* glory in that I did not run my race in vain or spend my labor to no purpose" **Philippians 2:16. AMP**

You will not finish your race without the right nutrition. You will get tired, worn out, fall behind, and eventually fall out. His Word is LIFE and TRUTH. Devour God's Holy Word like your life depends on it. It is water to your soul. His Word will equip you for this life. His Word is relevant, and it is for today.

The Word of God is coming under a heavy attack from the world today. I have heard it is "no longer relevant," or the writers' of His Word "didn't understand our society." How about this one: "It was written by man, not God." Blah, blah, blah. Settle this truth in your heart right now: The Bible was written by God through men. It is truth, life, and it is relevant. Period.

Ask yourself this question: *Without the Bible, how do I know who Jesus is?* The whole Bible, Genesis to Revelation reveals Jesus. If it is not the Jesus of the Bible, then it is not Jesus the Messiah, the Holy One of God.

> "Knowing this first, that no prophecy of Scripture is of any private interpretation, for prophecy never came by the will of man, but holy men of God spoke as they were moved by the Holy Spirit" **2 Peter 1:20-21. NKJV**

> "Every Scripture is God-breathed (given by His inspiration) and profitable for instruction, for reproof *and* conviction of sin, for correction of error *and* discipline in obedience, [and] for training in righteousness (in holy living, in conformity to God's will in thought, purpose, and action), ¹⁷ So that the man of God may be complete *and* proficient, well fitted *and* thoroughly equipped for every good work" **2 Timothy 3:16-17. NKJV**

I have a friend who runs marathons. One of the first marathons he ran, he didn't drink enough water. Throughout the miles, people would give him cups of water, but instead of drinking the water he poured it over his head to cool off. He got within yards of the finish line and he collapsed. His body was completely depleted of water and caused his muscles to fail. He eventually made it across the finish line because he crawled to the end. Yes, he finished. But, if you talk to him, he would rather have finished running strong.

You cannot run on empty. I practice fasting as a regular discipline in my spiritual walk. I try to fast one day a week, usually liquids only. Throughout the year, I try to do water only fasts, these are good for disciplining your flesh and, if you are in bondage to food, it will break you of that bondage. I did a ten-day, water-only fast one time, and I tried to go for my daily runs. It worked the first couple days, but after that, my body was having nothing to do with any kind of run. I could walk and my body thought that was okay, but as soon as I tried to run it just shut down. I was completely on empty, like a car trying to go with no gas in its tank. This is what happens when you are not spiritually filled up with the Word of God. You will flat-out die and give up the next time your enemy comes up against you.

This life is hard. If you do not take care of the physical body, you will be in and out of the doctor's office and on and off medicine trying to put a bandage on a gaping wound. Such it is with your spirit. Feed your spirit good food.

> "For the word of God is living and active and full
> of power [making it operative, energizing, and
> effective]. It is sharper than any two-edged sword,
> penetrating as far as the division of the soul
> and spirit [the completeness of a person], and of
> both joints and marrow [the deepest parts of our
> nature], exposing and judging the very thoughts and
> intentions of the heart" **Hebrews 4:12. AMP**

You cannot put a spiritual bandage on a gaping heart wound. You need to apply the Word daily to your life, let it heal your heart and mind. Let the Word bring encouragement and conviction. Let it do its job, so you can finish your race strong and whole, not weak and wounded.

Chapter 4

Running Blind

"What is blind running?" It's exactly what you think, running with your eyes closed. Does this sound dangerous to you? I suppose it could be very dangerous, if you were running down the middle of the road with a blindfold on (yes, very dangerous indeed).

I prefer to run outdoors almost always, but on occasion I will hit the treadmill at the gym. I like to pray when I run, and the televisions in front of me are almost always a distraction. Usually, some talk show will be on and I'll get sucked in, reading the ticker tape on the bottom wondering, *Who is that baby's daddy, anyway?* And before you know it, I've wasted a good forty minutes of prayer time. So, what I've found that works for me is to close my eyes, hold on to the front of the treadmill, and just go for it. I get in a rhythm, it's safe as long as I hold on and keep my pace up. I know the belt will continue to run at the speed I set and as long as I hold on, I won't slip and lose my footing.

Now, I tried this method one time running along my route through my neighborhood. I just wanted to close my eyes and press into God, but I kept running into the middle of road. There were no boundaries to keep me on my path and out of danger. I had to keep my eyes open to stay on track. This was not about me lacking faith, however.

"Now faith is the assurance (the confirmation, the title deed) of the things [we] hope for, being the proof of things [we] do not see *and* the conviction of their reality [faith perceiving as real fact what is not revealed to the senses]" **Hebrews 11:1. AMP**

Faith is blind, but it is not boundaryless. We have two boundaries that when we step out with our eyes shut, keep us on the right path. These are the Word of God and the Holy Spirit. So, running on the streets with my eyes closed wasn't a test of faith, after all.

Too many people "step out in faith," but refuse to stay within God's boundaries and end up in the middle of the road with a Hummer bearing down on them. This is dangerous.

You can run fast and far, not knowing where you are going or even how far you must go when the Holy Spirit is your guide. This is His job: to teach and guide you. And faith will get you there, but you need to keep your eyes on Jesus and your spirit fueled.

"But the Comforter (Counselor, Helper, Intercessor, Advocate, Strengthener, Standby), the Holy Spirit, Whom the Father will send in My name [in My place, to represent Me and act on My behalf], He will teach you all things. And He will cause you to recall (will remind you of, bring to your remembrance) everything I have told you" **John 14:26. NKJV**

"But when He, the Spirit of Truth (the Truth-giving Spirit) comes, He will guide you into all the Truth (the whole, full Truth). For He will not speak His own message [on His own authority]; but He will tell whatever He hears [from the Father; He will give the message that has been given to Him], and He will announce *and* declare to you the things that are to come [that will happen in the future]" **John 16:13. NKJV**

You should never step out in faith without the leading of the Holy Spirit. It is dangerous. You cannot go running blindly down the middle of the road. But, when He speaks, go for it! Get on that treadmill, grab onto Him, hold on tight and run. Don't worry, He'll supply the steps under you; you just have to move. Stay within your boundaries and obey God's Word. You do not want to get out of His will, and His Word is His will. Do you want great faith? Then Obey His word. Do you love Him? Then obey His Word.

> "Jesus answered, 'If anyone [really] loves Me, he will keep My word (teaching); and My Father will love him, and We will come to him and make Our dwelling place with him. One who does not [really] love Me does not keep My words. And the word (teaching) which you hear is not Mine, but is the Father's Who sent Me'" **John 14:23-24. AMP**

The boundary between walking in faith and being blessed is OBEDIENCE. Do you want to do GREAT THINGS for God? DO you want to preach the gospel? Heal the sick? Raise the dead? Then obey. It's simple, just obey. Even when you cannot see things clearly, you must obey. In *My Utmost for His Highest*, Oswald Chambers writes, "*You cannot think through spiritual confusion to make things clear; to make things clear, you must obey. In intellectual matters, you can think things out, but in spiritual matters you will only think yourself into furthering wandering thoughts and more confusion.*"

God has given you boundaries for your benefit. He wants you to be safe from the plans of the enemy. He wants to bless you and He wants to use you for His purposes!

> "If you will listen diligently to the voice of the Lord your God, being watchful to do all His commandments which I command you this day, the Lord your God will set you high above all the nations of the earth. And all these blessings shall come upon you and overtake you if you heed the voice of the Lord your God" **Deuteronomy 28:1-2. NKJV**

The meaning of "blessing" has been drastically changed in Christian circles. Somehow it has come to mean "more money and more stuff." This is not God's blessing. The word blessing is translated as "favor." Don't you want the favor of God? You need His favor in your everyday life. Favor with God and favor with men. Definition of favor in Merriam-Webster—*excessive kindness and preferential treatment*. Now, don't you want favor?

Yes, it is true. It rains on the just and the unjust. You will have good seasons and rough seasons. But, your circumstances do not change His favor in your life. You can have favor through the storm.

Two years ago, my friend's husband died unexpectedly. He had an aortic rupture, went through a fourteen-hour surgery, and died. While we were waiting to see if he was going to pull through the surgery, she and I were sitting on the floor crying. Despite the circumstances, she looked at me through tear stained eyes and said, "No matter what, I want to always praise Him." Those were powerful words. I told her, "Because that is your heart, then you will." He died and we left the hospital praising and worshiping the

Lord with all our hearts, tears streaming down our faces.

She sought to obey God and His will. The Lord moved on mine and Matt's heart to take her and her son in. Favor. We housed them. Favor. We fed them. Favor. We walked with them through the valley of the shadow of death. Favor. God gave her, and her son favor because she chose to always praise and obey Him no matter what, and He showed her favor. God completely and totally took care of her and her son in every realm. He supplied friends. He supplied a family. He supplied her money. And later, He supplied her with a house, a job, and eventually a new husband. Favor.

I know other people that have gone through the same thing, and forsook God. They got angry at God. They cursed God. They ran away from God. They were out of His presence and His favor. They didn't dwell in His presence. Where do you dwell?

> "He who dwells in the secret place of the Most High
> shall remain stable *and* fixed under the shadow of
> the Almighty [Whose power no foe can withstand]"
> **Psalm 91:1. AMP**

God hasn't changed. His Word hasn't changed and it's still as relevant.

> "Jesus Christ is [eternally changeless, always] the
> same yesterday, today, and forever" **Hebrews 13:8. AMP**

Faith and obedience go hand in hand. You cannot have one without the other. They are inseparable.

"But without faith it is impossible to please *and* be satisfactory to Him. For whoever would come near to God must [necessarily] believe that God exists and that He is the rewarder of those who earnestly *and* diligently seek Him [out]" **Hebrews 11:6. AMP**

"Are you willing to be shown [proof], you foolish (unproductive, spiritually deficient) fellow, that faith apart from [good] works is inactive *and* ineffective *and* worthless" **James 2:20. AMP**

James is not talking about works as a means to earn your salvation, but rather a work that proves your faith as when Abraham proved his faith by offering Isaac on the altar. My friend proved her faith when she sought after and obeyed God. Obedience proves that you have faith. Without obedience, the Bible says your faith is worthless. Do you see the connection?

I can look back on my life over the last twenty-two years of living in Christ and see the hand of God with me, even in that valley of the shadow of death. I have learned to embrace my valleys because His presence goes with me and builds my faith for my next "valley experience." I have learned to say, "Thank you, God, for this storm. Thank you for this challenge, because I know it is going to build my faith and I will emerge victorious on the other side."

If you are constantly avoiding the valley, you are never realizing the comforting presence of the Master. It is easy to praise Him and have faith when you are on the mountaintop, but what about the valley? However, it is in the valley that your most high faith is built as you learn to rely on Him to lead and guide you, as you lean on His unchanging hand and strength.

How deep is your faith? Is it ankle deep? Go knee deep. Is it knee deep? Go waist deep. Is it waist deep? Go neck deep. I believe that He would have you in the deep of the ocean, where your feet cannot touch the bottom in your faith.

It's time to grow your faith! What are you waiting for? Get on, *hold on*, close your eyes, and run blind!

Chapter 5

A Runner Dresses to Run

What you wear during exercise matters. You should never wear a skirt and sensible heels to go running. Forget the heels, you should not even run in jeans and Converse tennis shoes! If you are going to do any form of exercise, you must first figure out what the proper attire for that exercise is.

I do not preach to my women a lot about attire. I was saved in March of 1995 in a legalistic Pentecostal Church. I met God at that altar and I grew where I was planted. That denomination puts a lot of emphasis on clothing and what's considered "modest." Women could only wear dresses or skirts, and they had to be below your knees in length.

I was a baby Christian—that being my introduction to God and also wanting to work in various ministries in the church, I obeyed. I would see other women wearing skirts so tight you could see every curve and line, and I thought to myself, *How is that different than wearing pants?* These ponderings I kept to myself and let my questions go up to the Lord as I looked to His Word.

Four years later when I met my husband Matt, he wanted me to wear jeans. He not only wanted me to, he begged and pleaded with me to wear jeans, and so he went out and bought me a pair. I never felt uncomfortable wearing jeans, only that I might get "caught" by someone in my church and be taken out of my ministry. It is true, I would be removed from my ministry if I violated the clothing regulations.

I was wearing shorts one day (long shorts, mind you, down to my knees) while I was mowing my lawn. I lived in San Antonio and it's ninety-eight degrees in the shade if you're lucky. A neighbor up the road who went to a different Pentecostal church than I did, ran and told their friend, who told someone else, who told someone else, who told my pastor, "Sister Crystal is mowing her lawn in shorts." I was told that because I was a new convert and still learning, it was okay this time, but I was warned not to do it again. Now, I love my home church. I love my pastor and have made many lifelong friends there. I did not ever use my beliefs against their beliefs as an excuse to turn away from God, or stop loving on the people, or as the reason to leave the church and fellowship with another Body of Christ.

Like I said, I don't put a lot of those restrictions on the women in my church. Everyone grows at different rates and if you try to make someone holy from the outside, it never works. They must first have the Holy Spirit on the inside. He makes us holy, but it's a process. For some people who are moldable and teachable, the Holy Spirit can move fast. These people get it. They want to be changed. But for others, it is a slow, drawn-out process because they are hard-headed. Because we can all be hard-headed at times.

For some people, it takes a lifetime to receive the spiritual gifts of God, and for others they can accept it all as standard in a day. Modesty is one of those things that is hard to define. What's modest for me, may not be modest for you. Something

I wear can look completely different on you, and while it may flatter me and look professional and conservative, it might be something you would never wear

I knew one lady that harped on modesty all the time. To her, modesty meant always wearing dresses. One Sunday, she wore a dress to church in which the neckline came down between her breasts and when she turned sideways, the sides of her breasts were exposed. It was distracting, not to mention confusing.

That is why I don't harp on how women dress. Cover up the parts that need to be covered and let the Holy Spirit do His job. He's a good discerner. He will let you know if there is something you should not be wearing (that is, if you will listen). I praise God I have a godly husband that helps me in my attire. He lets me know when I wear something that could put a stumbling block in front of my fellow brother.

However, that's not exactly what I am referring to. As a runner, I dress to run. I wear a running bra, light pants and a light jacket, and running shoes. Now, as a runner you cannot wear just any old shoes. You have got to have good shoes. I wear Brooks Adrenaline. They're great running shoes with nice comfort and arch support. Me being me, I got tired of the boring colors of the Brooks and thought I would venture out and try some brightly-colored, visually-appealing Nikes.

At first, these shoes were pretty good. But, after about a month, I began getting shin splints and having trouble with my IT band. It got so bad, I had to stop running and switch to a bike. A bike is okay, and spin classes are fun, but I don't get the same workout. I don't get the same "runner's high." After about ten days of biking and stretching, I went back to running wearing my Nikes. This time, on the first run, my IT band seized up, and the pain traveled immediately into my lower back. *What the heck?* I began praying and asking God for the answer (because He says to pray about all things). He told me it was my shoes. The very next day I wore my old Brooks and there was no more pain.

What you wear running makes a huge difference in the health of your body. As it is with our physical body, so it is with our spiritual.

We need to get dressed spiritually every day for this world's battles. We cannot survive without putting on the right armor of God.

"Put on God's whole armor [the armor of a heavy-armed soldier which God supplies], that you may be able successfully to stand up against [all] the strategies *and* the deceits of the devil. For we are not wrestling with flesh and blood [contending only with physical opponents], but against the despotisms, against the powers, against [the master spirits who are] the world rulers of this present darkness, against the spirit forces of wickedness in the heavenly (supernatural) sphere. Therefore put on God's complete armor, that you may be able to resist *and* stand your ground on the evil day [of danger], and, having done all [the crisis demands], to stand [firmly in your place]. Stand therefore [hold your ground], having tightened the belt of truth around your loins and having put on the breastplate of integrity *and* of moral rectitude *and* right standing with God,

> "And having shod your feet in preparation [to face the enemy with the firm-footed stability, the promptness, and the readiness produced by the good news] of the Gospel of peace. Lift up over all the [covering] shield of saving faith, upon which you can quench all the flaming missiles of the wicked [one]. And take the helmet of salvation and the sword that the Spirit wields, which is the Word of God. Pray at all times

(on every occasion, in every season) in the Spirit, with all [manner of] prayer and entreaty. To that end keep alert and watch with strong purpose *and* perseverance, interceding in behalf of all the saints (God's consecrated people)" **Ephesians 6:11-18. AMP**

I do this every morning during my prayer time. I put on the whole and right armor of God.

I start with the helmet of salvation. This helps me to remember that I am in a right relationship with the Lord. You have been saved and you are a different person. Your salvation is secure in Him, so start with your helmet of salvation.

Next, I attach the breastplate of righteousness. I am the righteousness of God in Christ Jesus, as are you. You are not who you used to be. You are who God says you are. You can do what God says you can do. You are dead to sin and alive in Christ. You are His righteousness. Beautiful!

Then I "gird my loins with the belt of truth." Men of old "girded their loins" in preparation for battle. Get prepared to battle the enemy with the truth! I speak this every morning: "Your Word is truth. Your Word have I hid in my heart that I might not sin against you. Blessed are You O Lord, teach me your statues." His Word is truth. It's the only absolute truth on this earth.

Then I "shod my feet with the gospel of peace." This is the gospel of salvation. You are to be spreading His gospel everywhere you walk. You have to be about "your Father's business" in all that you do.

Next, I take the shield of faith. How big is your shield? You can have a small shield and maybe you'll be able to defend against a few arrows. But, wouldn't you rather have one of those Braveheart full body shields, so all you have to do is duck a little when the enemy is raining down on you with everything he's got? Yeah, that's how big I want my faith! Don't you want faith to move mountains, heal the sick, and raise the dead? That's the kind of faith I want. The faith to trust God to open the Red Sea when the enemy is fast-approaching from the rear. I want to have big faith in a great big God!

Lastly, take the sword of the Spirit, that Word of God coupled with prayer in the Spirit and use it! If you never get in the Word, you will not be able to use your sword. This and your shield are your offensive weapons. All the other armor is for defense from the enemy, but the sword is to go on the offensive, along with your shield, and take down the enemy by his Word. This is how Jesus overcame Satan in the wilderness, "It is written."

> "And the tempter came and said to Him, If You are God's Son, command these stones to be made [loaves of] bread. But He replied, It has been written, Man shall not live *and* be upheld *and* sustained by bread alone, but by every word that comes forth from the mouth of God" **Matthew 4:32-4. AMP**

Put on your armor every day. When I say every day, I mean every day. Satan is always on the prowl to find the weakest sheep. Don't let it be you! Your armor is a necessary thing if you are going to overcome and take down the enemy. Don't step out of the house without your armor on!

Irish thriller author Joanne Clancy said: *"Be the kind of woman who, when your feet hit the floor in the morning, the devil says, 'Oh no! She's up.'"*

I want to be *that* woman. I want to be a woman like Deborah, full of wisdom and unyielding courage, a God-ordained judge and prophetess of Israel, who went with the military leader Barak into battle to chase down Israel's enemy. I want to have the strength of Jael, just a common woman, no special gifts or anointing was said to be upon her; yet, she rose up and killed God's enemy with a tent peg. Sir, do you want to be a Joshua—a commander of the next generation to take down the giants that have stolen God's promises? Or a mighty man and servant of the Lord like Caleb? Because of his faithfulness to God in the wilderness, at the age of eighty-five said, "Give me that mountain and I will kill all those giants who stand in my way!"

We have a great many warriors to look up to. What about David, who came against the Philistine warrior Goliath with just a sling and stone but in the mighty name of the Lord? How about Elijah, who stood against a whole army and a slew of false prophets? Pick a warrior to emulate. These warriors of God went out dressed in their spiritual armor and slew their enemies, and *you* have access to this same armor. Put it on! What are you waiting for?

Chapter 6

Nine Minutes
at a Time

Do you remember having to run the mile in junior high school? What was your time? You probably had to run around the baseball field and then wait behind the back stop, taking a break until the next round of kids came through, right? My PE coach was oblivious, or maybe she just didn't care. The first time I ran the mile was in seventh grade. It took me a good fourteen minutes, and I was sucking air like a fish out of water. It was a hot, muggy spring day in Texas and I was seriously out of shape.

I've come a long way since then. Now, I run about a nine-minute mile. I'm good with that. In my younger years, I was way more competitive; but I have nothing to prove anymore. On colder days, I will go to the gym and run on the treadmill. The treadmill is not my favorite; most of the equipment at my gym is older and well-used, so the belt slips a lot. The only thing to look at is the television right in front of me. Occasionally, I'll watch people working out on the machines down below. Quite frankly, it's boring, stuffy, and smelly. The treadmill makes me feel like I'm in one of those hamster wheels, going round and round, doing nothing, going nowhere. But, on those twenty-nine-degree days, it certainly is a lot warmer. I find it much easier to give up on the treadmill. I set goals, but it's just too easy to stop and just "be done with it." I'm goal-focused, which is why I prefer to run outdoors. However far I run out, I have to run back that same distance.

This one day, I set for myself a goal of running five miles on the treadmill. I was jogging along, doing fine, praying to the Lord, and after four miles I just wanted to quit. I heard the Lord speak softly to me, "My daughter, just take nine minutes at a time. You can do anything for nine minutes." I began to weep. It's true, I can do anything for nine minutes. I've been through a lot of bad stuff in my life. I know what it's like to go without food, not just be hungry; but to literally have no food. I know what's like to be left alone to fend for myself, get myself up and ready for school, make my own breakfast, lunch, and dinner (when there was food). I survived being dragged from place to place. I lived in twenty-three different places by the time I was sixteen. In one year, I attended four different schools. From a very early age, I was taught the harsh reality that "Life does not revolve around me, at all." But, I survived. I got through it, nine minutes at a time. I believe that God created humans with the ability to endure *any* hardship, it is in our very DNA to endure. Yes, *you* were created to endure! Look at what Paul wrote to his son in the Lord Timothy:

> "But you have carefully followed my doctrine, manner of life, purpose, faith, longsuffering, love, perseverance, 11 persecutions, afflictions, which happened to me at Antioch, at Iconium, at Lystra what persecutions I endured. And out of them all the Lord delivered me. 12 Yes, and all who desire to live godly in Christ Jesus will suffer persecution"
> **2 Timothy 3:10-12. NJKV**

"You therefore must endure hardship as a good soldier of Jesus Christ" 2 Timothy 2:3. NKJV

Therefore, how much more should we be able to endure through the strength of the Spirit of the Living God? I think often we faint and give up because we get tired, and because the path at hand seems daunting and overwhelming. Take it nine minutes at a time. You were created to endure.

We get so caught up in this world, so completely goal focused we forget to take it nine minutes at a time. God may give you a great, big vision and ministry; but it takes time to get there. You have to take it nine minutes at a time. Your circumstances may seem completely overwhelming, just take it nine minutes at a time. You are not even promised tomorrow.

"So do not worry *or* be anxious about tomorrow, for tomorrow will have worries *and* anxieties of its own. Sufficient for each day is its own trouble" Matthew 6:34. NKJV

Jesus is not saying you cannot prepare for the future; He merely is saying you cannot get so wrapped up in the worry and anxiety of your tomorrow. You need to stay focused on doing what He has called you to—right here, right now. It's way too easy to get sidetracked by the difficulty of a five-mile run. Sometimes, that goal seems too lofty, too far out of your reach, especially if you are worn out and tired. Just take it nine minutes at a time.

I have a young friend who went to Ranger school. He was visiting with Matt and me when Matt asked him about how difficult was it. He said, "It's the hardest thing I've ever done." Matt then asked, "So how did you get through it?" He said, "I told myself every day that I would quit tomorrow. Then I'd get up the next day and say the same thing—'I'll quit tomorrow.'" He said this to himself every single day and it got him through the sixty-one days of training. If my friend can do anything for a whole day, the rest of us can get through anything nine minutes at a time. However, it still takes a "persevering" attitude. An attitude that says, "I'm going to do this. I will make it through this, even if it's nine minutes at a time." In other words, set your face like a flint!

> "For the Lord God helps Me; therefore have I not been ashamed or confounded. Therefore have I set My face like a flint, and I know that I shall not be put to shame" Isaiah 50:7. NKJV

Like Jesus going to the cross, set your face like a stone that cannot be moved and whose purpose cannot be thwarted. After all, you were created to endure.

> "Therefore, my beloved brethren, be firm (steadfast), immovable, always abounding in the work of the Lord [always being superior, excelling, doing more than enough in the service of the Lord], knowing and being continually aware that your labor in the Lord is not futile [it is never wasted or to no purpose]" 1 Corinthians 15:58. AMP

You can do this. There is no person or no devil in hell that can stop you. Set your goal. Set your face like a flint and do not stop and smell the roses. You got this!

I was out on my run and there was a lady running on the other side of the street. She came to a pretty rose bush and she stopped to smell the flowers. Now, she was already struggling on her run and she probably just need an excuse to stop. That's all well and good if you are running around your neighborhood. I don't know if she ever finished her run.

I know, I know. People say, "Stop and smell the roses" but on this marathon run of your life you cannot let anything distract you from finishing your race, not even pretty smelling flowers! Satan will throw distractions at you right and left; they may even look and smell pretty. But if you stop, you will get distracted from your run and the plan and purpose that God has for your life. Maybe that distraction is only for a moment, but it can become for a lifetime. Beware of distractions!

You *can* run this race. Set your face like stone that you will not be distracted from God's goal. Take it nine minutes at a time.

Chapter 7

It Doesn't All Depend On You

One of the best ways to be diligent in any type of exercise or exercise program is to get yourself an accountability partner. A partner will, hopefully, hold your feet to the fire. They will call you up and check on you to make sure you will meet them in the morning for your exercise time. They will be in your face when you missed an "appointment" with them. And, if they're a really good partner, they will not let you get away with any of your excuses. I have always been self-motivated. I was the kid who always wanted to work alone on my projects for fear that someone else was going to slow me down or not work to my standard. I have never really needed an accountability partner in order to run; I will run with or without you. But I make a good partner for someone else who needs that motivation.

We have a responsibility to God to discipline our minds and our flesh, but the rest depends on Him. He supplies the grace. He supplies the strength to endure. He will build your faith. He will carry you when you're tired and weary. He supplies the peace and joy. Even if you are self-motivated, you need some help in this area. The Holy Spirit is your running accountability partner. Trust me, you need His Spirit.

I get massive relief from stress when I run, partly because of the endorphin release, but also because I pray the whole time. If you happen to catch me running around the neighborhood, sometimes you'll see me crying. Sometimes you'll see me laughing. Occasionally, you'll see me yelling at something. And if you roll down your window, you'll hear me putting the devil in his place. I pray in the Spirit and I pray with my understanding. I pray for myself and my family, and I pray for my neighborhood. I pray.

God will take all your burdens, if you let Him. You can do all the things I tell you to do in this book, but be legalistic about it and miss the mark. What do I mean? The children of Israel were faithful to follow certain aspects of the law, but their heart was not connected to what God was asking of them. They were merely "rule followers" who continually bent the rules. They did not serve and obey the Lord from a position of love for Him and a surrender to Him. You must have a change in the desires of your heart and mind in order to experience true victory. Rule following won't cut it. You need the Holy Spirit to help you. He is your Helper. He is your Comforter. He is your Teacher. Use these tools, but allow God to move and have His way. Allow the Holy Spirit to lead you into all truth. He's good like that. He will lead you, guide you, teach you, convict you—it's His job! Let Him do His job.

"But the Comforter (Counselor, Helper, Intercessor, Advocate, Strengthener, Standby), the Holy Spirit, Whom the Father will send in My name [in My place, to represent Me and act on My behalf], He will teach you all things. And He will cause you to recall (will remind you of, bring to your remembrance) everything I have told you" John 14:26. AMP

God is a *good* God. He is longing to be your strength. He is longing to love you. He is longing to help you. He is longing to uphold you. He never fails. You will fail. God never fails.

Most days, my husband does not feel like running. He doesn't love it like I do. He really actually hates to run. He says the Army ran every ounce of "the joy of running" right out of him. But, he also knows the benefits. On a good day, he will get out there and run a good three miles just because he likes the sun on his face. And he doesn't mind running when the weather's perfect. However, when it's cold and rainy, it's a completely different story. That's when my diligence kicks in for him. He only goes because I'm going with him. He will suffer through the cold and rain, as long as I'm by his side.

> "Have I not commanded you? Be strong and of good courage; do not be afraid, nor be dismayed, for the Lord your God is with you wherever you go"
> **Joshua 1:9. NKJV**

He goes with you. When it's raining and cold out, He goes with you. When you can't do it alone, He goes with you. When you don't want to do it, He goes with you.

> "Even though I walk through the [sunless] valley of the shadow of death, I fear no evil, for You are with me; Your rod [to protect] and Your staff [to guide], they comfort and console me" **Psalm 23:4. AMP**

Did you know that the definition of "grace" changed after Jesus rose from the dead? Before Christ, under the Old Testament it meant "unmerited favor." I have heard people also define it as—*not getting what you deserve.* "Grace" under the New Testament became the word *charis*, which is defined in the Greek and translated thus in The New Strong's Exhaustive Concordance of Bible as—*the divine influence on the heart, and its reflection in the life.* I have done a lot of research on this word "grace" and many Biblical scholars believe that Paul actually changed the definition of "grace" after the death and resurrection of Jesus because he was so moved by the power of the cross. Grace is an action word. Grace is a power word. It is so much more than just pardon for your sins. It is the power and ability to overcome! It is the power of the Holy Spirit coming into your life. Action! Power! Grace is life changing! After receiving His grace, you are *not* meant to stay the same. This is why He told Paul, "My grace is sufficient." It is enough.

> "For the grace of God (His unmerited favor and blessing) has come forward (appeared) for the deliverance from sin *and* the eternal salvation for all mankind. It has trained us to reject *and* renounce all ungodliness (irreligion) and worldly (passionate) desires, to live discreet (temperate, self-controlled), upright, devout (spiritually whole) lives in this present world, Awaiting *and* looking for the [fulfillment, the realization of our] blessed hope, even the glorious appearing of our great God and Savior Christ Jesus (the Messiah, the Anointed One), Who gave Himself on our behalf that He might redeem us (purchase our freedom) from all iniquity and purify for Himself a people [to be peculiarly His own, people who are] eager *and* enthusiastic about [living a life that is good and filled with] beneficial deeds" **Titus 2:11-14. AMP**

I think it's interesting–and can be frustrating–to watch how some people attempt to change His grace into something it's not, and try to then "explain" to me what grace really is. I know His grace. I am familiar with His grace on a level some people have never experienced and for that I wake up grateful every day–it helps me run my race. I have received His grace. I have felt the depths of His grace come into my soul to heal and restore. I was so far down in a pit that I could not look up. I had done some truly despicable things in my life. I recall the time I performed sexual favors for modeling jobs, and found myself inches from being sucked into a prostitution ring when I was eighteen. I have done things that I cannot even mention. They are so horrible I wish I could forget. I flirted with disaster and evil on every corner. Wretched. Miserable. Destitute. But here's the crazy part: He knew the whole time and He still *chose* me. He chose to extend His beautiful, lovely grace to me and forgive me. And not just forgive me, forget my sins and never hold them against me, never. If not for His grace, I shudder to think where I would be. Are you in the pit of despair and destruction?

> "He drew me up out of a horrible pit [a pit of tumult and of destruction], out of the miry clay (froth and slime), and set my feet upon a rock, steadying my steps *and* establishing my goings" **Psalm 40:2. AMP**

Not only does He rescue you from the pit, He cleans you up and then sets you on high! What a gracious magnificent God! So, I ask you: have you truly received His grace? If your life hasn't changed, then I wonder? Do you want Him to go with you? Scratch that...you *need* Him to go with you! Let Him lead you down His path.

To be successful as a runner in this race, you are going to have to trust God's plan no matter how good something else looks or seems. The devil is really good at sending you the counterfeit all dressed up in a pretty package with a bow on top. For a runner, insoles can make a world of difference. I went down a nearby runner's store to buy the insoles I usually use. They no longer carried them. They wanted to "make" me a pair by molding their own insoles to my feet. That seemed legit. I took the time and let them mold me a pair of insoles. I put them in my shoes and walked around for a while. I jogged a little bit and jumped. I then asked the assistant how much they cost, to which she answered, "Eighty-two dollars." Yikes! My old ones were half the price. For this amount, I better feel like I'm walking on clouds, but these new ones didn't feel much different than the insoles that came with my shoes. I told her, "No, thank you," and I walked out. I went home and began looking for insoles online and reading reviews. Dr. Scholl's active series inserts kept popping up on different runners' sites as a good set of insoles for the type of running I do. So, I went to Walmart and got a pair for $19.99. I put them in my shoes, walked around for a little while and I immediately felt a nice improvement from the old insoles. The next day, I went for a run in them and they felt great. They gave me arch support, cushion on the balls of my feet, and shock support for my ankles. And they continued to feel great as the weeks went on. Good ole Dr. Scholl's insoles were all I needed. Now, would the insoles that cost $82.00 work great? Based on my dry run in the store, I can't imagine so, but I know they wouldn't be better than the ones I purchased for a reasonable price. Not everything that looks better is better.

I see this a lot in people's lives. they get distracted easily by Satan because he likes to use flash and bling to keep you from

God's plan. Just because something "appears" to be right and "seems" to make sense in the natural, doesn't mean it is God's plan. In my experience, God's path is the one less traveled. It is the high road where the air gets thin and it's difficult to breath. The devil makes his way "appear" beautiful. After all, he appears as an angel of light, but in the end that path is destruction. If you are going to run with God, you have to stay on His path and trust that it is the best path, no matter what it looks like.

Chapter 8

Competitive Running

It's not what you think. Well, maybe it is what you think! Do you know someone who has to win at everything? You know, the people you hate to play board games with because they can't just win, they have to crush you! You know the type. I know the type because it's me! (Do not play Monopoly with me; it will end in disaster.)

I'm pretty competitive, but Ranger is highly competitive. It's the funniest thing I've ever seen! I take him on runs through our neighborhood or out on my favorite trail and he'll be trotting along, until he spots another dog ahead of him. He breaks into a sprint until he catches up with the other dog, and then he prances by the other dog until he's ahead of that dog, and then he returns to his normal pace. It makes me laugh. Ever seen the movie *Seabiscuit*? He's a little like that horse—he has to be in front and he likes the competition. He is a funny dog.

When I'm on the trail, I feel like Ranger. I don't like to be behind people. I like to be in front and I will race to get ahead of them. Or if I'm at the gym running next to someone on another treadmill, I will look over to see how fast they are going and I will speed up my treadmill. I know it's childish, and that person doesn't even know or care what I am doing, but it's my own insecurities. If I can run faster and farther, then I feel better about myself. *I may not be faster than "that gal," but at least I beat the eighty-year-old man at the gym,* I think to myself proudly. Maybe it's just me, but I think a lot people compare themselves to others.

This is a dangerous game to play when you start comparing yourself to and competing with your brothers and sisters in Christ. What good is it?

> "Not that we [have the audacity to] venture to class or [even to] compare ourselves with some who exalt *and* furnish testimonials for themselves! However, when they measure themselves with themselves and compare themselves with one another, they are without understanding *and* behave unwisely"
> **2 Corinthians 10:12. AMP**

We are told that when we compare ourselves to another, we are without understanding and behave unwisely. Comparison is the mark of a person who does not know who they are in Christ. Comparison happens when you take your eyes off Jesus and unto others and your circumstances. You may ask questions like: Why are they blessed and not me? Why do I have to go through this and not them? Why do they always have money and not me? Why doesn't God use me like He uses them? Why can't I have their same gifting?

Have you ever asked these questions? I have. And then God showed me this scripture and it changed my life:

> "But Peter turned and saw the disciple whom Jesus loved, following the one who also had leaned back on His breast at the supper and had said, Lord, who is it that is going to betray You? [21] When Peter saw him,

he said to Jesus, Lord, what about this man? ^{22} Jesus said to him, If I want him to stay (survive, live) until I come, what is that to you? [What concern is it of yours?] You follow Me" **John 21:20-22. AMP**

Peter was just told by Jesus, "Feed My sheep. You are going to suffer for me, Peter." So, Peter looks at John and says something I would have said, "Lord, what about him? What are you going to do with him? What's he going to do? Will he have to suffer too?" I can hear it now—"Why me and not him!?" Or maybe it's the other way around—"Why him and not me?" Do you hear it? Do you see it? Jesus says those same words to you today, "Son, daughter, don't worry about what I do with anyone else. You follow me and do what I have told you to do. You *only* answer to me. Your anointing is specific to you! Don't compare yourself to *anyone*. Your scales are imbalanced."

You can get so off-track when you play the comparison game. I tried for years to be someone else. I tried to teach Bible study the way others taught Bible study. I tried to preach like other preachers. I tried to fellowship like others fellowshipped. I tried to love like others loved. It didn't work. It never works. Matt is a very demonstratively loving man. He is gregarious and outgoing. He loves to talk and connect with people—anyone, anywhere, at any time. It is who he is. It is who God created him to be. Right after my son was born, we were living in Copperas Cove, TX and flew to California to visit with Matt's father. On the return flight, we were delayed in Dallas because of bad weather, and eventually we got stuck in Dallas for the night. Matt was chatting it up with the airline worker, like he usually does, and I tried to chime in. He was an older man, possibly in his fifties, and his nametag had his first and last name displayed. Trying to be like my husband, I said something funny and called the man by his first name. This is something my husband always does, but it back fired on me. The man immediately corrected me, "My name is Mr. Richards." Boy, my face went flush. I was so embarrassed and I apologized profusely for being disrespectful. Somehow, when it comes out of Matt's mouth, it is loving, but apparently not when it comes out of mine. I've tried numerous times to be like Matt, but I'm not him. God didn't create me to be him. God doesn't want me to be him. I am me.

You are you. God created you to be you! He loves your boldness and He will use it. He loves your shyness, and He will use it. He loves your ability to give, and He will use it. Whatever gifts you have, God gave you those gifts and He wants you to use them for His purpose. You are not anointed to be someone else. You are anointed to be you. There are a lot of people out there who will have their opinion on what you should be, how you should act, how you should share the gospel, how you should love; but His opinion is the only one that matters.

Listen to the voice of your Beloved. "You are mine."

> "But now [in spite of past judgments for Israel's sins], thus says the Lord, He Who created you, O Jacob, and He Who formed you, O Israel: Fear not, for I have redeemed you [ransomed you by paying a price instead of leaving you captives]; I have called you by your name; you are Mine" **Isaiah 43:1. AMP**

> "And I will cause you to pass under the rod [as the shepherd does his sheep when he counts them, and I will count you as Mine and I will constrain you] and bring you into the covenant to which you are permanently bound" **Ezekiel 20:37. AMP**

You don't have to compare yourself to anyone. You don't have to compete with anyone. He loves you, with all your faults and all your inconsistencies. He formed you for His purpose. He made you for His pleasure. Allow the Holy Spirit to refine you, but don't allow others to change you. YOU ARE HIS!

Theodore Roosevelt coined the phrase "Comparison is the thief of joy." Amen to that! Comparison is a killer. It will rob you of all peace and all joy and replaces those things with depression and discouragement. On "that day", you will stand before the judgment seat of Christ alone and will give an account for only you and whether or not you did what the Lord asked.

> "For if anyone thinks himself to be something, when he is nothing, he deceives himself. But let each one examine his own work, and then he will have rejoicing in himself alone, and not in another. For each one shall bear his own load" **Galatians 6:3-5. NKJV**

So how do you overcome comparison? I'm glad you asked! Here are a few ways I use: 1. Know WHOSE you are whom you are in Christ. You were created by Him and for Him. Your purpose is to bring Him glory. 2. Live for an audience of One. Don't be a people pleaser. The vertical relationship is the most important. 3. Give it away. When I get discouraged, I give away encouragement. It gets the focus off me. 4. Realize you have no idea what they did to get where they are. You see the beautiful ballet dance, but can't see their gnarled toes under those ballet shoes. 5. Be grateful for what He has done in your life. I don't deserve anything but judgment, and He gave me grace. 6. There's no one like you! Why would you want to be someone else? I pray this helps you overcome comparison, in Jesus's name!

Chapter 9

You Don't Always Have to Feel Like It

You're about one-third of the way through this book and probably thinking, *Man, this lady loves to run! And she loves talking about running! She must always feel so excited to run.* To that, I laugh. That couldn't be further from the truth. In fact, a lot of days, I definitely, most adamantly, do not feel like running, at all. No way. However, I run. Like your spiritual walk, running is a discipline of the flesh.

I run because I know that after I am done, I always feel better. I have more energy. I get my blood pumping, and I feel alive. If I start the day with a headache, usually from my sinuses, it's gone after my run. Running clears the head, both figuratively and literally clears out my sinuses. But, most days it's hard to be motivated to get out there and run, especially if it's rainy and cold. I go anyway. I don't have to feel like it, I just do it because I know it's what needs to be done in order to feel better. A runner runs.

This is the walk in the Spirit. Ever hear the saying, "The Spirit is willing, but the flesh is weak"? The flesh will consistently and constantly fight against the Spirit. Therefore, the things of the Spirit do not come easily or willingly. You must exercise the Spirit. Crucify the flesh and feed the Spirit. Especially in those areas and on those days, you "just don't feel like it." Loving the mean hearted. Forgiving those who do not repent but continue to hurt you. Showing mercy on the merciful-less. Giving grace to those who use and abuse you. It is what you are called to do—*even if you do not feel like it.*

This is the age we live in. People are led by their emotions. As a follower of Jesus, you must be led by the Spirit.

> "For all who are led by the Spirit of God are sons of God" Romans 8:14. **NKJV**

He tells, you to FORGIVE or you will not be forgiven. Ouch! When do you ever feel like forgiving someone who has hurt you badly?

> "But if you do not forgive others their trespasses [their reckless and willful sins, leaving them, letting them go, and giving up resentment], neither will your Father forgive you your trespasses"
> **Matthew 6:15. AMP**

Notice Jesus doesn't say, "Forgive, but only if you FEEL like it."

My mom was "radically saved" about two years before I came to the Lord. I was about twenty years old. We never had a relationship; it was a tolerated one at best. I lived in Tennessee at the time, trying to find my worth and value following around a man. I watched my mom from a distance. She talked differently. She walked differently. She dressed differently. She completely stopped drinking. She went to church. She went to Bible study. She prayed. It was weird seeing my mom this way, but I could not deny that something awesome and wonderful had taken place inside her and she was being transformed into something beautiful. Watching my mom be transformed by the power of God was like watching my mom suddenly rise and walk after being confined to a wheelchair her whole life. It was miraculous. Because we were estranged, my mom knew not to pressure me, but rather she prayed for me. I know that it was my mother's prayers that brought me to the Lord. When He forgave me, I had to forgive my mom. She didn't even ask me to forgive her, but I just knew I had to. At that time, I didn't feel like forgiving her, but He told me to forgive her. So, I chose to forgive. It was a long process of renewing my mind and every day choosing to forgive her. It did not come easy at first, but the more I chose to forgive, the easier it got and pain and bitterness began to melt away. My heart softened towards my mom, but the feelings of genuine love and forgiveness came *after I forgave*, not before. It's amazing how that works. If I can forgive the person who hurt me the most in my life; then I can forgive anyone. Forgiveness is powerful.

He doesn't say, "Love. But only if you feel like it."

> "He who does not love has not become acquainted with God [does not and never did know Him], for God is love" 1 John 4:8. AMP

Ouch! That one hurts. Are you a mean person? You need to start loving. How can a child of God walk around mean, sour-faced all the time, telling people off, picking fights with other Christians and still claim to love God? God says you can't. How do you know if you are mean? Do people avoid you like the plague? Do you have any long-standing relationships? Do you go through friends like a hot knife through butter? If you answered "yes, no, yes," well then, "Houston, we have a problem." This agape love that we are called to have is a love that is willful and with purpose. It is not a "touchy, feel good" love. You do not have to "like" someone in order to agape love them. It is not this mushy false love that just accepts and tolerates everything. It is the love spoken of in John 3:16, "For God so *agaped* the world." It was with *purpose and sacrifice* that He sent His Son. Agape love is a willful love of the heart and mind. It voluntarily suffers inconvenience and discomfort. Agape love chooses to show kindness and mercy, even when you do not like someone and expect nothing in return. It does not mean that you tolerate sin because you are "just supposed to love." You can "love" someone all the way to hell because you are fearful of man and his reprisal. According to 1 John above, if you do not agape love, sacrifice to the point of discomfort, you do not know God. Agape love turns people from their sin to Jesus. Are you turning people to Jesus? Are you loving with purpose and sacrifice? Love does not rejoice in iniquity (sin), but rejoices in the truth. Love bears all things, believes all things, hopes all things, endures all things. Agape love never fails.

Jesus tells you that with whatever measure you give something out, you will receive it back.

> "Give, and [gifts] will be given to you; good measure, pressed down, shaken together, and running over, will they pour into [the pouch formed by] the bosom [of your robe and used as a bag]. For with the measure you deal out [with the measure you use when you confer benefits on others], it will be measured back to you" **Luke 6:38. AMP**

You can give out love, grace, mercy, truth, forgiveness—and you will get it back. But, you can give out hate, unkindness, unforgiveness—and that is exactly what you will get back. The world calls this "karma," but God's Word simply calls it "reaping and sowing."

> "Do not be deceived *and* deluded *and* misled; God will not allow Himself to be sneered at (scorned, disdained, or mocked by mere pretensions or professions, or by His precepts being set aside.) [He inevitably deludes himself who attempts to delude God.] For whatever a man sows, that *and* that only is what he will reap. For he who sows to his own flesh (lower nature, sensuality) will from the flesh reap decay *and* ruin *and* destruction, but he who sows to the Spirit will from the Spirit reap eternal life"
> **Galatians 6:7-8. AMP**

I remember going through a rough patch early in our ministry, the kids were young and still in diapers. Matt worked full-time at an outside job and we had just planted the church, which needed his and my full attention. We had one vehicle, which Matt needed, and so I was home all day with the children in a townhome that we were renting. We were not bringing in much money, and I had no friends or family to speak of around me. I was running a Bible study in my home, and so ladies would come over every Thursday morning and fill up the parking lot. I had a neighbor who did not like this. People would park in the area she wanted for her cars, even though it wasn't marked as such, and she would come and yell at me all the time. That winter, I happened to earn some extra money and bought myself a jacket that I absolutely loved. It was denim with a fur collar and was a longer length so it looked a little more "dressy" than a regular denim jacket. I was so excited! I had not bought myself anything in a few years. I brought it home and was trying it on in the mirror and distinctly heard the voice of the Lord speak to me, "Give it to your neighbor." What?! No?! It couldn't be His voice! He wants it for me! All these things ran around in my mind as I argued with the Lord. I didn't feel like giving this mean person my new jacket. But I did. I swallowed my pride, remembering what Jesus did for me on the cross and I wrapped the jacket in Christmas paper, went over to her house and gave her a present. I said to her, "The Lord wants me to tell you that He loves you." And you know what? I never heard her complain about parking ever again. She didn't come to the Lord on that day, but I believe I planted a seed.

CHOOSE to sow to the Spirit. Choose to forgive, even if you don't feel like it. Choose to be kind, even if you don't feel like it. Choose to love, even if you don't feel like it. Then, *after*—you will feel great!

Chapter 10

Run Where
He Leads You

Where is your favorite place to exercise? Heck, maybe you hate exercise! Then, where is your favorite place to "just be"? Do you like to "get away" and clear your mind?

My favorite place to run is an outdoor trail that cuts through a forest of beautiful deciduous trees and curves along a creek. It's about ten miles from start to finish. It's a beautiful trail, no matter what the season. It's pretty secluded; therefore, Matt doesn't like me to run it by myself. As a husband, he wants to protect me. I get it. When I lived in San Antonio, I used to run at night, by myself. After the sun went down was pretty much the only time it was cool enough to run. I was never afraid.

I went running last week on the trail alone. Before I left, I prayed and asked God if it was safe. He gave me peace and the go ahead. I had a great run. Matt came home and I told him I went by myself. At first, he was worried, but I reassured him that I sought wisdom first and I asked God. He said, "I guess I'm okay with that. God knows better than me."

I don't operate in fear—anymore. When I was a freshman in high school I was estranged from my mom and lived a state away with some friends in New Mexico. This was one of the worst years of my life. The family I lived with had two daughters, one my age and one older. The eldest daughter became pregnant the year I lived with them and, well, I was to blame. I was the "bad influence;" therefore, I had to be removed.

I didn't want to go back to Texas and so I moved in with another family in the area whose daughter was a friend. This other friend had dropped out of school as a freshman and stayed up all night partying and sleeping all day. I tried to juggle the partying and getting up early for school, but it didn't work. We began hanging out with a group of guys who were Satanists. Yes, real, live, worship-the-devil, pentagram drawing, witchcraft-spell-casting Satanists.

In fact, one of the guys was growing marijuana using his own blood and urine as fertilizer. True story. I hung out with these guys most of the year, went to parties with them, and saw some crazy stuff. One time, I witnessed a boy rolling around on the floor, convulsing, eyes rolling back into his head, and foaming at the mouth in the middle of a party. Crazy things.

The girls and I were cruising the town one night and saw a vehicle we recognized at Baskin Robbins, so we pulled in. Two of the Satanists came out, spoke something in a demon tongue, and I felt something jump on me. (Yes, demon speaks in tongues. Satan has nothing new under the sun, but to mimic the beautiful works and manifestations of the Lord and the Holy Spirit.) I don't know what he said, but something—fear—jumped on me like an allergic reaction and didn't let go.

After that day, every thought and action was one of fear. I begin having heart palpitations and panic attacks. I would take my pulse every day all day, because I thought I was going to die. This is the spirit of fear. It is a strong spirit and it is destructive and crippling. I was fourteen and started to drink heavily to numb the fear.

At one point, I bought a Rottweiler and had him sleep with me—with the door shut and bolted, a dresser placed in front of it, and a gun beside my bed. Crippling fear. It's a horrible spirit and its real. "Get rid of it now!" A tiny voice begged.

> "For God did not give us a spirit of timidity (of cowardice, of craven and cringing and fawning fear), but [He has given us a spirit] of power and of love and of calm and well-balanced mind and discipline and self-control" 2 Timothy 1:7. AMP

I remember the day I was born again. I began to see things differently. It was like my whole life I had been looking through foggy lenses and suddenly someone has cleaned them for me. But, the spiritual battle was still real. That spirit of fear I had been nursing for so long did not like the Holy Spirit, and it fought me hard. I had demonic apparitions appear to me in the middle of the night and fear would return, until I learned to battle it.

> "The seventy returned with joy, saying, Lord, even the demons are subject to us in Your name! And He said to them, I saw Satan falling like a lightning [flash] from heaven. Behold! I have given you authority *and* power to trample upon serpents and scorpions, and [physical and mental strength and ability] over all the power that the enemy [possesses]; and nothing shall in any way harm you. Nevertheless, do not rejoice at this, that the spirits are subject to you, but rejoice that your names are enrolled in heaven" Luke 10:17-20.

There is *power* in the name of Jesus! You have power and authority in and through His name. His name carries the power and authority to heal the sick, raise the dead, cast down demons; through His name you can overcome any thing the devil throws at you. You don't have to walk in fear. You can run on that beautiful trail alone. You can go where He calls us you to go, and do what He calls you to do when He calls you. If the Holy Spirit lives inside you, you can run where He calls you to run and you don't have to fear. Fear will keep you focused on your failures and everything negative. To run your race, you must focus on your victories. I remember watching an interview with Peyton Manning. The interviewer asked him why he never seems to get frustrated and lose his poise, especially when he throws an interception. He said he just lets it go, every time. Every play is new. You cannot focus on your failures, you have to look ahead to the victory.

Is it hard for you to not focus on your fears and failures? Guess what? God will help you with your weaknesses.

> "Likewise the Spirit also helps in our weaknesses. For we do not know what we should pray for as we ought, but the Spirit Himself makes intercession for us with groanings which cannot be uttered" **Romans 8:26. NKJV**

My dog, Ranger, has a weak stomach. Not just sometimes, but a lot of times. Poor guy. If he eats too much too fast, it's coming back up. If he drinks too much too fast, it's coming back up. If he runs too hard, it's coming back up. If he gets too excited, it's coming back up. You get the picture. But, we know this about our dog. He's had a weak stomach since he was a puppy. When this happens, we don't yell at him and scold him for having a weak stomach. We just clean up after him and try to make him feel better. In fact, we have so grown accustomed to this weakness that when we hear him about to lose it, one of will run for a towel, or Matt will sacrifice his t-shirt. It's a dirty job, but someone's got to do it.

Guess what? Jesus isn't scared of a dirty job. He knows your weaknesses and He longs to help you as your High Priest.

> "Seeing then that we have a great High Priest who has passed through the heavens, Jesus the Son of God, let us hold fast our confession. 15 For we do not have a High Priest who cannot sympathize with our weaknesses, but was in all points tempted as we are, yet without sin. 16 Let us therefore come boldly to the throne of grace, that we may obtain mercy and find grace to help in time of need" **Hebrews 4:14-16. NKJV**

HE WILL HELP YOU, IF YOU LET HIM! With His help, you can conquer fear and failure. With His help, you can do *all* things. He takes all your excuses off the table. You can run where He leads you when you cast off fear and move forward in faith. But, you have to look to Him to help.

I struggled with anxiety and panic for many, many years. Since I was delivered, I have counseled women who deal with these anxiety issues. They all have the same common trait: they try to "stay busy," running to everything and everyone, instead of the only one who can actually help them. They "stay busy" doing stuff, even ministry, as I did. They will run to the therapists, as I did. They will run to drugs, as I did. They will run to other people, as I did. I had a therapist that put me on Paxil, stating, "It's the only thing that will help." Instead of listening to the Holy Spirit, I went on Paxil, and it caused some damage to my nervous system when I weaned myself off it. I had the worst withdrawal symptoms. I was in the 4–10 percent minority that experience horrific symptoms. It was horrible, and it almost ruined my marriage.

It wasn't until God gave me a vision of me attacking that spirit of fear through the Holy Spirit that I was able to overcome it. He showed me that He had already given me the power to overcome, but I wasn't drawing from it. I began vehemently attacking that fear with the help of the Holy Spirit and the Word of God. I would focus in on Him and let everything else fade away. I stopped going to others, and would come to Him immediately for strength, reminding myself that He gave me power to overcome my enemy of fear. I did not let up until it was gone. I was persistent and because I didn't quit, because I faced that fear time and again, I haven't had a panic attack in years.

You, too, can overcome fear in Jesus's name. His Word declares it, and you never again have to be afraid to run your race!

Chapter 11

Peace Like a Pool

Do you need more peace? Heck, I have never met anyone who said, "Not me! I'm good in the peace department. Give it to some-one else." Nope, never once have I heard those words. Whenever I think of peace, I think of those old Calgon commercials from the eighties: "Calgon, take me away!" Yes, you need peace.

You already know by now that I dislike running on the tread-mill. Maybe that's your "thing," but it's not mine. But, if I must go to the gym, I like a specific treadmill. Most of the belts slip on a lot of the treadmills, but there is a certain one that overlooks the pool that doesn't slip. I like this specific treadmill. Plus, I like to watch the ladies in the pool doing their water aerobics while I'm running. It gives me something to focus on other than the television. I'm not a big television watcher, there is never any-thing good on anymore. Remember the *Dukes of Hazard*? or The *A-Team*? That was my kind of programming! If I must, I'll watch ESPN at the gym and catch the sports highlights.

I was at the gym a while back and running on my favorite treadmill, overlooking the pool. It was a beautiful sunny day, and the sun was shining unto the pool through the large gym windows. The windows are about 12x12 and there are three of them. As the light was shining in, the thin slat of wall between the windows was casting a beam-like shadow across the water. At this time, there was no one in the water; it was completely still and at peace making the shadows from the beam easy to see. The shadow spread across the water from one end to the other and from my distance it appeared as if I could walk across the beam over the water.

I'm praying in the Spirit, as I like to do while I run, and the Lord spoke to me, "Watch the beam, Crystal. While the water is at peace, you can walk across that shadow beam, but watch the water."

Right after that, someone entered the pool and slowly that beam began to move. "Watch the beam, Crystal." Another person entered the pool and my beam began to zigzag back and forth like crazy. Another person got in, and another and another. With all the splashing and swimming around within a minute, my beam was completely gone.

This is what happens when you take your focus off Jesus and onto your surroundings. You lose your peace. As long as your eyes stay focused on Him, you can walk across that shadow beam. But once you start focusing on the people swimming around you, you lose your beam. You cannot walk safely on it. It becomes nonexistent. You will drown.

He doesn't just give peace. He *is* peace.

> "You will guard him *and* keep him in perfect *and* constant peace whose mind [both its inclination and its character] is stayed on You, because he commits himself to You, leans on You, *and* hopes confidently in You" Isaiah 26:3. AMP

Notice the words "whose mind is stayed on You." You have to keep your mind focused on and stayed on Him; that is if you want to be at peace. What you focus on will become magnified. How big is your God?

I heard it once said that if you have a big God, you have little problems. But if you have big problems, you have a little god. Again, it's what you focus on and you have a big God!

It never fails to amaze me how many people limit God. How do you limit a limitless God?

> "Behold, I am the Lord, the God of all flesh; is there anything too hard for Me" **Jeremiah 32:27. NKJV**

This is of course a rhetorical question. Why will you magnify your problems? Why not MAGNIFY God? You serve the God who parted the Red Sea and had His people walk through on dry sand You serve the God who made the sun stand still. You serve the God who caused the walls of Jericho to smash so hard to the ground that they actually went into the ground! How's that for a BIG GOD?

One of Satan's greatest weapons is to steal your peace. Make no mistake, Satan is very good at his job and his job is to steal, kill, and destroy. He is after you and he never fights fair. He will kick in the face when you are down. We think we are in a boxing match with the devil, but there are rules to a boxing match. He is in a street fight. He does not fight fair! Peace does not come easily, therefore, it must be sought after. Pursue peace.

> "Let him turn away from wickedness *and* shun it, and let him do right. Let him search for peace (harmony; undisturbedness from fears, agitating passions,

and moral conflicts) and seek it eagerly. [Do not merely desire peaceful relations with God, with your fellowmen, and with yourself, but pursue, go after them!]" **1 Peter 3:11. AMP**

I remember when my grandmother died. It was a real shock. I happened to be in Michigan at a friend's wedding, and I had left her in good hands. She was just fine on the day I departed. Two days later, my mom called to tell me grandma was in ICU hooked up to a machine because she had an ulcer that perforated, leaked into her blood system, and shut down all her major organs.

Immediately after the wedding, I flew back, landed in San Antonio, and went to her bedside with all these thoughts circling in my head. *I am losing the lady who was always there for me. The one who I spent every summer with and who took me camping, to Disneyland, to the beach, to the lake. The woman who taught me how to cook and to keep a house; how to wear makeup. The woman that said, "You never leave the house without lipstick and mascara."* And then the questions came: *What was I going to do? How would I live without her? Where would I live? What job could I get?* She was in bad shape, I didn't recognize her because her body was so bloated. She hadn't moved in days. I asked the Lord to help me and to help her. I sat beside her and grabbed her hand, "I'm here, Grandma. It's Crystal". She opened her eyes and looked at me and squeezed my hand. She had been hanging on and waiting for me to get there before she died.

Peace came flooding over me. She was in the Master's hands and so was I. I didn't have to worry about anything. He would take care of me.

You see, God does not give peace in the sense of "world peace." It's not the peace where everybody gets along and sings, *"I'd like to teach the world to sing in perfect harmony"* and we

74

drink a Coke and smile. No, it's a peace between you and God. It's the ability to boldly enter His presence as His child. It's a peace that says, "I have you in My hands, Child. I will handle this. I got this. Do not worry."

> "Peace I leave with you; My [own] peace I now give
> *and* bequeath to you. Not as the world gives do I give
> to you. Do not let your hearts be troubled, neither
> let them be afraid. [Stop allowing yourselves to be
> agitated and disturbed; and do not permit yourselves
> to be fearful and intimidated and cowardly and
> unsettled.]" **John 14:27. AMP**

Do you hear Jesus? Stop *allowing* yourself to be agitated and disturbed! Do not *permit* yourself to be fearful and intimidated! Do you hear Him saying, "Focus on me!"?

If you do not pursue peace in His presence, you will fall into the "victim mindset." Your problems will become too big for you and you sink into a pity-party of selfishness, which says, "Nobody loves me. Everybody hates me. I'm gonna eat some worms. Woe is me!"

You may not have control over your circumstances, but you can control how you react to them. You can either give the devil a foothold and let him run havoc all over you, or you can choose to be at peace. You can choose to say, "God will take care of me through this. He has me. I am His and He will not leave me."

> "Looking away [from all that will distract] to Jesus,
> Who is the Leader *and* the Source of our faith [giving
> the first incentive for our belief] and is also its
> Finisher [bringing it to maturity and perfection].
> He, for the joy [of obtaining the prize] that was
> set before Him, endured the cross, despising *and*

ignoring the shame, and is now seated at the right hand of the throne of God" **Hebrews 12:2. AMP**

I mentioned in a previous chapter another scripture that has helped me so much in my life: "When my father and my mother forsake me, then the Lord will take me up" Psalm 27:10.

When I lived with my godmother in seventh grade, I asked her one day why my mom didn't want me or love me. My godmother replied that when I was born, I was the apple of my mom's eye, but somewhere along the way she lost track of me. She lost her path. See, even moms and dads can forsake their children. My life circumstances as a child are proof of that, but God has always had me in his hands, fully, tightly, and completely. Let me break this down for you:

God has you in His hands. Fully—*in every way, to the furthest extent, abundantly, without lack or defect. Tightly—fitting closely, especially too close, fixed or fashioned in a firm place, difficult to move, fastened, attached or held in position that is not easy to move. Completely—from the Latin "to fill up," having all parts, in every way, from beginning to end, not lacking anything.*

Does this give you peace? That He has you in His hands fully, tightly, and completely? Knowing this gives me peace. Maybe you have been forsaken by a mother or father. Maybe you are a mother that has forsaken her child. I am here to tell you that you can still find peace! It is not too late. He can still restore and bring peace to your family. He brought peace to me and my family. He brought peace and comfort to my heart and He brought peace to my mom. Now, I am no longer condemning my mom; in fact, I love her very much. I realized that she tried to fill that empty hole in her soul with drugs and alcohol and it consumed her life. She told me one time that she never felt loved by her mom and, right then, God gave me compassion for my mom. She'd tried to find her peace in a bottle.

What things are you allowing into your pool? What lies are you clinging on to? What holes in your soul are you trying to fill with the things of this world? Have you truly relinquished all things into God's hands? How peaceful is your pool? This race is so much smoother when you run in peace.

Chapter 12

Tackle the Hills

You probably don't enjoy walking uphill. You're in good company; most people prefer to keep it level when they're out for a stroll. Think about this for a minute: why don't you like the hills? You're probably answering my question out loud right now: "Because it makes me work harder and sweat more, silly!"

I like to run in places that have hills. For different reasons, I like to challenge myself and I like to raise my heart rate. Your heart is a muscle like any other muscle. It needs to be worked out. This is why most athletes will do "interval training," which is periods of a higher pace following a slow pace. Some people will do a run/walk interval. Others will run up a steep slope, or steps, and then turn around and walk down them. This is a great cardiovascular workout. For myself, I like to add a hill into my run and then I tackle it at full force. I push myself to run as fast as I can to the top. I have found in the past that if I take hills slowly, I lose momentum and end up walking, and like I said before, walking is failure for a runner, or at least a runner like me. Yes, there are times when we all need to slow down and walk, but not on my runs. I set out with a purpose and a goal, to *run* my distance. Hills can present a problem if I don't approach them with a positive attitude. It's the "I think I can" attitude. "I think I can, I think I can, I think I can," until I get to the top, and then it turns into, "I thought I could, I thought I could, I knew I could." I can then slow my pace a little, get back into my form, take a few deep breaths and get my breathing under control.

> How do you approach your problems? Your attitude and mindset have all do with your performance in life. We are told in Proverbs that as we think about ourselves, so we become. "For as he thinks in his heart, so is he" **Proverbs 23:7.**

Your "thought life" must be taken under control if you are to have victory in this world and over your circumstances!

> "Do not be conformed to this world (this age), [fashioned after and adapted to its external, superficial customs], but be transformed (changed) by the [entire] renewal of your mind [by its new ideals and its new attitude], so that you may prove [for yourselves] what is the good and acceptable and perfect will of God, *even* the thing which is good and acceptable and perfect [in His sight for you]" **Romans 12:2. AMP**

How do you expect to overcome anything without the right mindset? The Bible says that when you are born again you have access to the mind of Christ:

> "For who has known *or* understood the mind (the counsels and purposes) of the Lord so as to guide *and* instruct Him *and* give Him knowledge? But we have the mind of Christ (the Messiah) *and* do hold the thoughts (feelings and purposes) of His heart" 1 **Corinthians 2:16. AMP**

But, again, you control your thoughts. God does not make you do or think anything. Some thoughts originate with you, others from the Lord, and still other thoughts are put there by the devil. Just because the devil gives you a thought, does not mean that he can read your mind! This is a misconception. The devil is not all-knowing, all-seeing, and everywhere at once. He is not God, nor is he the exact opposite of God. He is a being that was created like every other angel. He has been given way too much credit. He will put thoughts in your head, but you control what you will do or won't do with those thoughts.

How do you know if a thought is from God or the devil? If it does not line up with the Word of God, then it is not from God. Period. His will always lines up with His Word. I heard a story from my old pastor about a lady who would always come forward for an unspoken prayer request. The second time she came forward for prayer, my pastor told her that he felt uncomfortable with her prayer request, as he wanted to know what he was praying for. She told him that God had spoken to her and that she was going to marry a man, who was already married; therefore, she was praying for that man's wife to die. Sounds pretty drastic, right? But, this stuff happens all the time to people that don't control their thought life. You will give heed to "seducing spirits" and miss the voice of the Lord.

This doesn't have to be as extreme as praying for the death of others. If you are constantly listening to the negative thoughts of, *You're no good. You can't do anything. Who do you think you are? Nobody even likes you anyway.* Then, you will not accomplish much. You can, and should be listening to His thoughts about you. *You are valuable. You are fearfully and wonderfully made. You are mine. You are the apple of my eye and I have a great plan for your life. You can overcome any hill set before you!* Take your thought life captive! Cast down every thought that is not from God immediately!

> "[Inasmuch as we] refute arguments *and* theories *and* reasonings and every proud *and* lofty thing that sets itself up against the [true] knowledge of God; and we lead every thought *and* purpose away captive into the obedience of Christ (the Messiah, the Anointed One)" **2 Corinthians 10:5. NKJV**

If you do not tackle evil thoughts immediately, they will move into your heart and then you become those thoughts, and act on those thoughts. *"As a man thinks in his heart, so he becomes."*

Or you can be proactive and get you a big dog! No, I don't mean like my old Rottweiler; I'm referring to Ranger, my companion and running buddy. Another good way to tackle the hills is to have a big dog that can pull you. This is, of course, my favorite way! A good dog will pull you up that hill lickity split! What is your purpose for getting a pet? We have always bought large dogs, mainly as a running partner. I had a Weimaraner when we lived in Texas who was a pro at tackling hills! I miss that dog.

Are you proactive (acting in anticipation of future problems) when it comes to tackling your hills? Or do you just respond after something happens? I find that most Christians, or rather most people these days, are either passive (do nothing), or they just wait until they hit their threshold and then respond. This is a bad idea. This creates a yo-yo effect in your life. Living in the land of responding never produces any good fruit and leaves you tired and weary, sometimes even a little hopeless.

You have to prepare for that hill. Proactive people stay full of the Spirit, prayed up every day. They are always in the Word of God. They don't skip church, Bible study, or small group or fellowship because proactive people know where their strength comes from. A proactive person has formed relationships in the house of God, and so they have reliable brothers and sisters to help them when that hill turns into a mountain and they need someone to drag them up it. The proactive person knows her weaknesses and calls out to God for strength—instead of doing it on her own—before she even gets to that hill. Did you know that He is Lord even over your hill?

I hate taking medicine. When I say "hate" I mean hate—with a passion. I am very sensitive to medication, even allergy medication. I am not sure if it is because of my past history with drugs, or just my body, but I refuse to take anything that alters my body. My husband gets so mad at me when I have a cold because I refuse to take any kind of cough or sinus medicine, and I just suffer through. I even had both my kids au naturel. I would rather feel the pain than numb my body or take anything that makes me feel weird. Last summer was rough. I spent the day at a water park with my kids and we stopped for ice cream on the ride home. While enjoying our cones, my heart fell into a weird, flip flop rhythm. Now, it had done this on several occasions in the past, but I was always able to get it back into its normal sinus rhythm. This time was different. Hours went by and my heart rate sped up like a panic attack, but in a crazy, unnatural rhythm. I ended up in the ER, where they shocked my chest three times get my heart back into its natural rhythm. I was diagnosed with Atrial Fibrillation (or AFib). After I went into AFib, my doctor prescribed me a beta blocker. I was mad about taking it. I cried out to God and threw a little temper tantrum because I did not want to take those heart pills. He spoke very clearly to me, "I am Lord, even over those pills." I broke down crying. He is Lord even over your greatest battles and biggest hills. You can run this race because He will give you the strength to get up that hill. Get ready to tackle it!

Chapter 13

Let the Dog Poop
Before the Run

I know what you're thinking, "She said 'poop'!"

I live in area where you have to pick up your dog's poop, as it should be. I don't like seeing doggy poop on the sidewalk or trail when I'm out running, as well as I'm sure others don't either. Ranger is a ninety-five-pound yellow lab. Now, I have found if I feed him breakfast when I first get up in the morning, he has time to eat and "do his business." But, if not, he ends up having to poop on our run. They have an extra strict "pick up your doggy's poop" policy on my favorite running trail—busy and well used. There are several other outdoor enthusiasts on the trail when I'm out there; bikers, runners, walkers and other dogs. Many times I have been on the trail, in the middle of my run, and Ranger has to go. So, I will take him off trail and let him poop in the woods. The Lord spoke to me concerning this, "Crystal, just because someone cannot see the poop does not mean it's not still there." Ouch! (There's a deeper spiritual lesson in this.)

We live in a time when people would rather "ask for forgiveness rather than permission." Unfortunately, this attitude has transferred over into our new life with Christ. We want to do "what we want, when we want," no matter the consequences, and then ask for forgiveness and act like it never happened. This is misusing the amazing grace that He died to give us. Grace is not just pardon, it is power. Power to overcome every obstacle, trial, and temptation that the devil can throw at us. He gives us grace and power to overcome, when we come to Him first.

"For because He Himself [in His humanity] has suffered in being tempted (tested and tried), He is able [immediately] [a]to run to the cry of (assist, relieve) those who are being tempted *and* tested *and* tried [and who therefore are being exposed to suffering]" **Hebrews 2:18. AMP**

He wants you to run to Him first—before you fall into sin. He promises to give you the strength to overcome, because oftentimes what happens when you fall into sin is you hide it in the dark and are ashamed. And like Adam, you become, once again uncomfortable, in His presence.

"But the Lord God called to Adam and said to him, 'Where are you?' He said, 'I heard the sound of You [walking] in the garden, and I was afraid because I was naked; and I hid myself'" **Genesis 3:9-10. AMP**

Yes! There is forgiveness when you fall back into sin, but why would you not want the victory? Sin brings shame and destruction. You can absolutely be forgiven from any and all sin, but sometimes that sin leaves lasting effects on your life. Read the story of King David if you don't believe me. God always provides a way out, but you don't always want to take the way out. Sin appears so beautiful in the beginning. Satan himself is transformed as an angel of light; therefore, sin is going to look pretty good. Sometimes, it can even masquerade as being godly, but in the end, it bites. Wouldn't you rather avoid being bitten altogether?

Sin is bondage and there are many warnings in scripture about "returning to the bondage" that God brought you out of.

> "For if we go on deliberately *and* willingly sinning after once acquiring the knowledge of the Truth, there is no longer any sacrifice left to atone for [our] sins [no further offering to which to look forward]. [There is nothing left for us then] but a kind of awful *and* fearful prospect and expectation of divine judgment and the fury of burning wrath *and* indignation which will consume those who put themselves in opposition [to God]" **Hebrews 10:26-27.**

These are *real* and *literal* warnings from the Holy Spirit about returning to a life of sin. Why does God hate sin so much? Because He is a Holy and Righteous God and sin separates you from His presence. You cannot approach God if you live in habitual, unconfessed sin. He longs for you to be in His presence. He longs for you! It grieves Him when you sin. In essence you are saying, "I choose this sin over You, God."

This is one of my biggest pet peeves in the Christian world: the idea that we have to continue to sin. I've heard all the excuses: "I'm not perfect like Jesus." "I'll always sin as long as I live on earth." "I have to sin." "I'm just a sinner."

A sinner is someone who lives in their sin. They get up every morning preparing to sin. They don't know anything different than "to sin." Their heart is set to sin. Their mind is set to sin. They walk and live in sin. It is their nature to sin.

"The one who practices sin [separating himself from God, and offending Him by acts of disobedience, indifference, or rebellion] is of the devil [and takes his inner character and moral values from him, not God]; for the devil has sinned and violated God's law from the beginning. The Son of God appeared for this purpose, to destroy the works of the devil" 1 John 3:8. AMP

Where does it say that once we are born again we have to continue to sin? In fact, the Bible states just the opposite:

"What shall we say [to all this]? Are we to remain in sin in order that God's grace (favor and mercy) may multiply and overflow? Certainly not! How can we who died to sin live in it any longer? Are you ignorant of the fact that all of us who have been baptized into Christ Jesus were baptized into His death? We were buried therefore with Him by the baptism into death, so that just as Christ was raised from the dead by the glorious [power] of the Father, so we too might [habitually] live and behave in newness of life" Romans 6:1-4. AMP

"Therefore, [there is] now no condemnation (no adjudging guilty of wrong) for those who are in Christ Jesus, who live [and] walk not after the dictates of the flesh, but after the dictates of the Spirit. For the law of the Spirit of life [which is] in Christ Jesus [the law of our new being] has freed me from the law of sin and of death" Romans 8:1-2. AMP

"Therefore if any person is [ingrafted] in Christ (the Messiah) he is a new creation (a new creature altogether); the old [previous moral and spiritual condition] has passed away. Behold, the fresh and new has come" 2 Corinthians 5:17. AMP

This was a hard concept for me for many years. I was told, "You are a sinner," and so I was at the altar every week repenting of any bad thoughts, when I wasn't out doing anything. I was a wreck week after week. We preach victory in Christ and "new creation," but continue to tell the righteous that they are still sinners. If you are told something long enough, you believe and eventually act on it. "As a man think in his heart, so he becomes." You *were* a sinner, but now! Oh, we forget the "but now."

> "And such were some of you [before you believed]. But you were washed [by the atoning sacrifice of Christ], you were sanctified [set apart for God, and made holy], you were justified [declared free of guilt] in the name of the Lord Jesus Christ and in the [Holy] Spirit of our God [the source of the believer's new life and changed behavior]" **1 Corinthians 6:11. AMP**

But now you are free from the stain of your sin. But now you are free from the guilt and the shame. But now you are a new creation, born again of God's seed, holy and blameless before Him. You are His righteousness.

> "For our sake He made Christ [virtually] to be sin Who knew no sin, so that in *and* through Him we might become [endued with, viewed as being in, and examples of] the righteousness of God [what we ought to be, approved and acceptable and in right relationship with Him, by His goodness]"
> **2 Corinthians 5:21.**

If you can get this down in your spirit, it will change you forever. Once the Holy Spirit comes in, you have a nature change. Now, your nature is His nature. It's a nature of righteousness.

"No one born (begotten) of God [deliberately, knowingly, and habitually] practices sin, for God's nature abides in him [His principle of life, the divine sperm, remains permanently within him]; and he cannot practice sinning because he is born (begotten) of God. By this it is made clear who take their nature from God *and* are His children and who take their nature from the devil *and* are his children: no one who does not practice righteousness [who does not conform to God's will in purpose, thought, and action] is of God; neither is anyone who does not love his brother (his fellow believer in Christ)"
1 John 3:9-10.

If you are born again, you are a new creation. You are no longer a sinner. Oh, you might sin, but a sinner abides in her sin. A righteous man falls, but gets back up and keeps on running. The righteous know who their Father is; they know Him by name. The righteous repent quickly and keep moving on. They are not hindered and dragged down by their flesh because they walk in the Spirit.

You cannot hide your sin either. He knows.

"So do not make any hasty *or* premature judgments before the time when the Lord comes [again], for He will both bring to light the secret things that are [now hidden] in darkness and disclose *and* expose the [secret] aims (motives and purposes) of hearts. Then every man will receive his [due] commendation from God" **1 Corinthians 4:5.**

If He knows all your pain and suffering, He certainly knows all your sin. He knows! This reality should bring you much comfort. You don't have to "hide the poop." You can just pick it up and deal with it properly, or you can prepare.

You can get up early, feed the dog before your run and seek God first. You can read your Bible every day and you can listen to the Holy Spirit and be quick to obey His voice. You don't have to fall back into sin. You have been given the strength and power to overcome.

"Besides this you know what [a critical] hour this is, how it is high time now for you to wake up out of your sleep (rouse to reality). For salvation (final deliverance) is nearer to us now than when we first believed (adhered to, trusted in, and relied on Christ, the Messiah). The night is far gone and the day is almost here. Let us then drop (fling away) the works *and* deeds of darkness and put on the [full] armor of light. Let us live *and* conduct ourselves honorably *and* becomingly as in the [open light of] day, not in reveling (carousing) and drunkenness, not in immorality and debauchery (sensuality and licentiousness), not in quarreling and jealousy. But clothe yourself with the Lord Jesus Christ (the Messiah), and make no provision for [indulging] the flesh [put a stop to thinking about the evil cravings of your physical nature] to [gratify its] desires (lusts)" **Romans 13:11-14.**

It's high time you lay aside every single weight that has the ability to hinder your run. Cast off and leave behind that old life of sin. Get rid of your negative and corruptive mindset. Do not open any door that is not of God and cover every crack that allows Satan into your life. Ask yourself these questions: "Are my friends influencing me for evil?" "Are the shows I watch and the music I listen to having a positive or a negative influence on my life?" "Am I participating in something that God has no place in?" "Are my thoughts and actions lining up with scripture?"

All these and more will weigh you down and you are in this race until the end. You still have a long way to go. To run fast and long, you're going to have to lighten your load.

Chapter 14

Have Good Form

Have you ever had leg or back problems? A lot back problems are due to bad posture and tight hamstrings. "Now you tell me," you say. Sit down and stretch out your hamstrings and feel your back loosen and relax. It works. Try stretching about thirty minutes a day and watch and see how your muscles relax.

Matt has always had lower back problems, but recently, they have gotten worse. He attributed his latest pain to needing new running shoes. Now, Matt does not run as often, or as far, as I do, so he doesn't need to purchase new shoes as regularly. (Yes, this might be a little jab—ha ha!) That being said, we both love getting a new pair of running shoes. It's like running on a cloud. However, he happened to talk to a physical therapist that told him the pain he was feeling was not from his shoes, but rather from his running form. The PT told Matt he needed to run completely erect, shoulders back, chest out, abs sucked in, and head held high. Do you remember the Olympics back when Michael Johnson competed? He was the man with the golden shoes. I loved watching him run. He had perfect form and he moved beautifully.

I have pretty good form, usually. I've been trying this "better form" running and it's not as easy as it would seem. It's hard to concentrate on keeping your shoulders back, chest out, abs sucked in, and head held high when you get tired. In the beginning it's not too bad, but the longer the run, the harder it is to keep good form. Yes, this is what Matt and I were now aiming for.

The other day I took Ranger on a run. He's getting old, I'm sad to say. He's nine and he just can't keep up like he used to. He used to be able to run five miles no problem, but now three miles is a struggle for him. Poor guy. So, I'm trying to have good form, it's the last mile and I'm tired, and then my dog begins to drastically slow down. So, there I am, trying to keep my shoulders back, chest out, abs sucked in, head held high, and I am literally dragging my nine-year-old, ninety-five-pound lab. No amount of "Come on boy, you can do it!" or tugging of his leash was going to cut it. I had to either lose the dog, or lose the good form. (I kept the dog, in case you were wondering.)

You cannot hold onto the things of this world and still expect to have the victory! You cannot live in this world and be in God's Kingdom. The two are contrary to each other. There are dead things that you need to let go of. The point here isn't that I need to lose the dog; to be clear the point is I compromised form to keep the dog. God is good with that, but He's not okay with us compromising our integrity, our judgment, our values in order to "maintain good form." Know the difference.

> "No one can serve two masters; for either he will hate the one and love the other, or he will stand by *and* be devoted to the one and despise and be against the other. You cannot serve God and mammon (deceitful riches, money, possessions, or whatever is trusted in)" **Matthew 6:24.**

What is holding you from having God's form? Is it a relationship? Is it money? Family? Stuff? Sin? Thoughts? You were created for so much more. God has a plan and purpose for your life, but you have to let dead things go.

> "Therefore then, since we are surrounded by so great a cloud of witnesses [who have borne testimony to the Truth], let us strip off *and* throw aside every encumbrance (unnecessary weight) and that sin which so readily (deftly and cleverly) clings to *and* entangles us, and let us run with patient endurance *and* steady *and* active persistence the appointed course of the race that is set before us" **Hebrew 12:1.**

One of the biggest and most damaging dead weights a person can carry with them is the victim mindset. You know the one. It's the one that says, "I can't do this because of that." It says, "You don't know." It says, "You wouldn't understand." You have to leave this thinking behind. It's not productive. It's dead weight.

When I came to the Lord, I was completely broke and broken. I had no money, no clothes, no car, no house, no job, no "stuff," no relationships, no value, no worth, no dignity. Nothing. Just me. That's all I could give Him was me, and He wanted me. He loved me. He cherished me. Just me. This heart-broken, sexually abused, misused, unloved, unwanted shell of a person—He wanted me. I had abused my body with drugs from age nine. I was sexually molested by different boyfriends of my mom's. I once had a knife held to me and was given drugs and made to perform explicit sexual acts on a woman, while she did unspeakable things to me. I was ten. I was so traumatized by this incident that I had buried it and forgot about it. I never believed in repressed memories until this one came rushing back after a movie that

Matt and I watched a few years ago. I was date raped as a freshman in high school. My mom constantly chose men and alcohol over me. I was shipped around. I would fall asleep in one place and wake up in another as young child. I was used and abused. I was married at nineteen to a man over the phone. (Yes, you can get married over the phone!) After two years, I had an affair and ran away with another man. I completely desecrated my body. I drank to numb my brokenness. I pretended like everything was okay. I put a fake smile on, while dying inside the whole time. Broken. Numb. Abused. Neglected. Unloved. Unwanted. I *was* a victim. But then....

> "Therefore if any person is [ingrafted] in Christ (the Messiah) he is a new creation (a new creature altogether); the old [previous moral and spiritual condition] has passed away. Behold, the fresh *and* new has come" **2 Corinthians 5:17.**

I was invited to church. He found me. He pursued me. I surrendered at the altar on a beautiful Wednesday night. The Holy Spirit came in and I was REVIVED and made ALIVE in Christ! I began spending hours upon hours in His Word and in prayer. I began memorizing Scripture. I wanted to know Him. I wanted to know His ways. I wanted to always be in His presence.

But, people told me I couldn't "do this" or "do that" because of my past. They put that old yoke back on me. I knew that God had a plan and a purpose for my life. I knew He had more for me than what others told me. I knew that if I listened to them and not to Him, I would go nowhere. I would remain in bondage. I would remain a victim. I listened to the Holy Spirit and applied the Word to my life in every area and I conquered.

"Yet amid all these things we are more than
conquerors *and* gain a surpassing victory through
Him Who loved us" **Romans 8:37.**

The phrase "more than conquerors" is one word in the Greek,
hupernikomen. Huper means—above, over. *Nikomen* means—vic-
tors, conquerors. Paul is literally saying that instead of victims
in a fallen world, you are over and above conquerors. You are a
super-victor!

God restored my life. He gave me my awesome and wonderful husband, Matt. He blessed me with two beautiful and amazing children, Gabriel and Faith. He called Matt and I to pastor
a church for Him. He placed me in a position of leadership and
authority. He did this, not me. I am not my past. I am not a victim. I am victorious in Jesus.

What is your story? Your story is history. Your past does not
define you. He wants to do amazing things in your life. He wants
to bless you in all heavenly places. He wants to make you the
head and not the tail. He wants to use you to fulfill His purposes.
He has a great plan for you.

"For I know the thoughts *and* plans that I have for
you, says the Lord, thoughts *and* plans for welfare
and peace and not for evil, to give you hope in your
final outcome" **Jeremiah 29:11.**

BUT, do you believe it? Will you receive it? Will you get rid of
every dead weight and run the race set before you?

"And I am convinced *and* sure of this very thing, that
He Who began a good work in you will continue until
the day of Jesus Christ [right up to the time of His

return], developing [that good work] *and* perfecting *and* bringing it to full completion in you" **Philippians 1:6.**

Get rid of your ways and your plans that hinder. Listen and obey the Holy Spirit. I remember being in my fourth year of college. I was preparing to go to physical therapy school. I applied at UT Health Science Center and passed my first two interviews. I had done 100 hours of volunteer work in the physical therapy dept. at Lackland AFB. I was studying for the GRE. I had a 4.0, was in the Laurel Wreath Honor Society, and in the Who's Who of colleges in the nation. Yep, I was on my way. And then God told me to quit college. "No way!" I screamed. "I am not doing that. This is *my* dream. This is *my* plan for my life." I fought for three weeks with God. I wasn't sleeping good. I wasn't eating. I was a complete mess. Then, I gave in, gave up, and quit school. Perfect peace. I remember sitting on the front pew on a Wednesday night for church and crying. My pastor came up to me. He asked me why I was crying. "I quit school because the Lord told me to and now I have no idea what I am going to do." I never saw such a huge smile on a man's face. He told me he was proud of me for listening to Jesus and that he wished more people would obey God like that. Great. But I still had no idea what I was going to do with my life.

Short story: If I hadn't quit school, I would've never been in the place to meet Matt. I wouldn't have met him, married him, had my children or started a church. Plain and simple.

Good form means laying aside everything He asks you to. Lay it aside and leave it behind. Good form means obeying His voice, down to the very last detail. Remember, He's intimately familiar with *His plans* for you, not your plans for yourself. Our plans can leave us in pain and disillusioned with God. Good form also means watching the words of your mouth.

Do not run with your mouth open! The other morning, I was running on the trail on a beautiful spring day, with birds chirping, flowers blooming, and the bugs were out in full force. I like to chew gum when I run, and I do mean "chew." I chew my gum like a cow chews the cud. So, there I am running along, chewing my gum and a big bug flies right into my mouth and gets stuck in my gum. So gross! I spit out my gum immediately. Note to self: *if you keep your mouth shut the flies won't get in.*

What are you speaking? Your words are powerful. Words are containers. Ever hear this: "Sticks and stones may break my bones but words can never hurt me?" Anyone that was called a name as a child—fatso, four eyes, cow, dog-face, and so on—knows that idiom is a lie. Those words can still sting, even as an adult we carry those words with us and let them continue to affect us. We are told:

> "Death and life are in the power of the tongue, And those who love it will eat its fruit" **Proverbs 18:21.**

You can speak *life* to your situation and circumstances, or you can speak death. You can speak God's Word over yourself and others, or you can speak doubt and defeat. I do not advocate the "just speak it, believe it, and receive it" theology, but I do believe what the Bible says about God's Word:

> "My son, give attention to my words;
> Incline your ear to my sayings.
> Do not let them depart from your eyes;
> Keep them in the midst of your heart;
> For they are life to those who find them,
> And health to all their flesh"
> **Proverbs 4:20-22.**

The Word is life! It brings healing and health to all your circumstances. It is powerful. Good form means speaking *life* and God is gracious enough to make sure His Word accomplishes that which He sent it to do.

> "For as the rain comes down, and the snow from
>   heaven,
> And do not return there,
> But water the earth,
> And make it bring forth and bud,
> That it may give seed to the sower
> And bread to the eater,
> So shall My word be that goes forth from My mouth;
> It shall not return to Me void,
> But it shall accomplish what I please,
> And it shall prosper in the thing for which I sent it"
> **Isaiah 55:10-11.**

Have good form. Let dead things and dead words go. Leave them behind. It is the best and only way to victory!

Chapter 15

A Successful Runner is Teachable

"You can't handle the truth!" I can see Jack Nicholson's mad face on the big screen screaming at us right now. For this chapter, you are going to have to be truthful with yourself. Teachable. Moldable. Shape-able. *Do these words describe you?* What about these words: rebellious, stiff-necked, hard-headed, unteachable? I'm not talking about once a in a while. On occasion, I have a tendency to be as stubborn as a mule; I get that. But I'm referring to the majority of the time. On most days, are you a teachable person?

Today, Matt and I went for our run and it was one of those rough, Monday mornings. I have to admit I ate too many gummy bears while watching Sunday Night Football. Too much sugar makes for a rough Monday. I know better.

Matt and I are working on having better form when we run, but like I said before, when I get tired, I lose good form. Instead of head high, shoulders back, chest out, abs in, my shoulders slouch, my head's down, and my stomach's out. Horrible form. I was sucking wind and was hoping to get in at least a three-miler without quitting. It was looking dim. Matt looks over at me and says, "Honey, watch your form. You're slouching." To which I replied, "I am?" I was too gummy-bear hungover to notice.

"Thank you!" I said, and immediately fixed my form. Interestingly enough, my body automatically felt better. My back and legs felt great/lighter and adjusting my form gave me more energy, so I was able to add another two miles to the route.

If you are not teachable, you will suffer badly. God puts people in your life to *help* you along your path. No one has "arrived" not me, not you, not even your pastor all by themselves. You will not "arrive" until you die and are in His presence. You should be constantly growing, changing, and maturing in the meantime. I think one of the saddest things is to see is a person who claims to have been a follower of Christ for twenty years, but they are still the same person from twenty years ago. They still act the same, think the same, do the same things because they "know it all" and they are not going to allow anyone to tell them what to do. You know the type. They have it all figured it; therefore, there is nothing you can teach them. I have to admit that when I met my husband, I was a lot like this: "Whoever loves instruction *and* correction loves knowledge, but he who hates reproof is like a brute beast, stupid *and* indiscriminating" **Proverbs 12:1.**

Matt had a lot of wisdom to give me, but I thought he was trying to correct me so he could "lord" over me. It took time and patience on Matt's part for me to see that he was trying to "help" not hurt me. He wanted me to be everything that he knew I could be.

Are you a scoffer? Do you jeer and mock? Do you treat people and new circumstances with contempt? Would others say you are a disagreeable and unpleasant person?

> "A scoffer seeks Wisdom in vain [for his very attitude blinds and deafens him to it], but knowledge is easy to him who [being teachable] understands" **Proverbs 14:6.**

These scoffers are the type that remain disconnected from the Body of Christ. Why should you go to church or be in relationship with others if you have it all figured out? The church is not a building, it is the Body of Christ. You need the Body as much as the Body needs you. God uses the people in the Body to refine us.

There is a runner's store near me. This is where my husband and I buy all our shoes. They have a system there where you run on a treadmill for a few minutes and they record it in order to help you find the best pair of shoes for your feet. I found out I pronate on my left leg and I have super-duper high arches. If I continue to run without fixing these problems, I will have some serious health issues later on in life. I was able to buy stability shoes and a high arch insert. It has *really* made a difference. I listened and it has helped me greatly. I could have said, "No thanks. Even though you know what you're doing and have even seen this problem a lot, I'm going to go with a cheap pair of shoes and continue to disregard my leg issues." How stupid.

God has placed people in your life in order to help you. It would behoove you to listen!

My daughter plays basketball. I know a family that keeps seeking a "winning team" for their "winning" daughter. They happen to have a daughter that has poor character; she's been called un-coachable. She's a ball hog, throws tantrums, talks back to the coach, rolls her eyes, ridicules her teammates when they miss a play, etc. She got a lot of ability, but her character is sorely lacking. And her parents have had a heck of a time finding the right fit for her. You see, no teams wanted her, despite the fact that she's got a high-scoring game and great ball handling skills. See, God cares more about your character than your ability. It was what Paul is trying to teach us in 1 Corinthians 13. "And though I have the gift of prophecy, and understand all mysteries, and all knowledge; and though I have all faith, so that I could remove mountains, and have not love, I am nothing." You can have all the gifts and abilities in full measure, but unless we are walking in a character that displays God's love, you are nothing. Character is refined through teaching and coaching. It comes through yielding your own selfish wants and desires. God uses others to refine you! I believe in my heart that if this particular player could have let go of her attitude and ego and listened to her coaches and modeled her teammates' behavior, she'd be a part of creating a winning team, rather than having to seek one out.

I recently preached at a women's event, and I could feel the spirit of a woman that wanted nothing to do with what I was preaching. It was as if every word bounced off her and boomeranged back at me. It grieved me. I thought, *Please just listen. This Word will help you. It will benefit you. It will change you if you let it.* There's no wisdom in being stiff-necked and rebellious. She was there, which meant she must have been there for a reason. Let me help you. Let others help you! Let others speak into your life. When you get off track, allow others to correct you and lead you back on the right path. This is wisdom. Confrontation always reveals character. What does this mean? It means that how you receive correction and reproof reveals whether you are teachable, or whether you're rebellious. There is no wisdom in being a rebellious person. Allow a brother or sister to sharpen you.

> "Let the righteous man smite and correct me it is a kindness. Oil so choice let not my head refuse *or* discourage; for even in their evils *or* calamities shall my prayer continue" **Psalm 141:5.**

Maybe you're just not comfortable going to church because you're an introvert. This is an excuse. I'm an introvert. I grew up alone. I am an only child and I was left to raise myself for most of my life, as you know. Because of that, I prefer to be alone. I like to be alone. I used to feel massive anxiety from being in any type of group atmosphere, and I'd suffer horrible, intense panic attacks.

When Matt and I were first married, we liked to be alone, spending time with each other, getting to better know one another. However, we'd have soldiers over all the time because Matt was an NCO. It was important to him, and to us, so we'd reach out to the young privates who were stuck miles away from home and we'd open our home to them. I have always been hospitable. I like to cook and serve—I'm kind of a "Martha" like that. But, having to actually sit and fellowship was a different story. This way—including the cooking and serving—made it easier for me to adapt to having company.

However, we started our church in 2003 with two other families, one of whom I barely even knew. I was forced to fellowship. Everything we did revolved around us and fellowship. We had parties and fellowship. We celebrated birthdays and fellowship. We watched football and fellowship. I was forced to fellowship. Slowly, I have been brought out of my shell, both by my husband and the Spirit of God. It is more than possible, if you let Him. If you choose to stay stuck in your corner, eating your nachos, then it's your own fault. You don't like those words, do you? You were not created to live this life alone. You were created to be in fellowship.

I still prefer to be alone, but I know that it is not God's will. Did you know the defining characteristic of an introvert is that we are energized by being alone? We can get exhausted fellowshipping. It does not mean we are shy, it just means we need to energize alone. Whereas extroverts get pumped up from being around others. If you are an introvert, stop using it as an excuse to not be a part of the Lord's Body.

> "And let us consider *and* give attentive, continuous care to watching over one another, studying how we may stir up (stimulate and incite) to love *and* helpful deeds *and* noble activities, Not forsaking *or* neglecting to assemble together [as believers], as is the habit of some people, but admonishing (warning, urging, and encouraging) one another, and all the more faithfully as you see the day approaching"
> **Hebrews 10:24-25.**

In case you were wondering, God healed me of my panic attacks and anxiety, but I had to step out first. The Israelites had to cross the Jordan in order to enter into the Promised Land. God led them through the Jordan, but the priests had to step out onto the water first.

You have to take every excuse off the table if you want to walk in victory. He will help you. He will give you the strength and grace to do it. And He will supply the people to teach you and help you along your path.

"But you don't understand. I've been hurt in church." Well, welcome to the club. First of all, there are a lot of people "in church" who aren't even saved. They can talk a good talk, but they don't know the Lord. Secondly, the church is full of hurt people—and hurt people, hurt people. I have been hurt and offended more times than I can count, but I have to stay. Matt and I are the pastors. I literally can't leave or abandon my job. Think about that for a minute. What if one Sunday you showed up to church and your pastor didn't show up because he was offended after the service he gave the night before? What if the worship team never came because they were hurt? How about the children's ministry teachers—if a child said something hurtful, should they stay home?

We live in a broken world with broken, hurt people. Why God has asked us all to come together, get along, and love each other is beyond me—but He did. Group settings teach you how to "work it out." They teach you how to apologize and forgive. They teach you how to not be easily offended and extend grace. God wants you to stay put and be used! Don't listen to the lies of the enemy—God wants you to be in the church and he wants to use you for his purposes! Get in and plant your roots and then get out there and get busy running!

Chapter 16

Runners Adopt Other Runners

Ever heard the phrase *like attracts like*? What you like to do and enjoy doing, you want others to experience with you. If you're a scrap booker, then (hopefully) you love to scrap book. Because you love to scrap book, you want others to experience that same love. If you are a donut eater like my honey, then you want others to experience the yummy goodness of a good donut. A donut eater will find another donut eater so that they can go out and enjoy eating donuts together.

For our first duty station form the Army, we moved to Copperas Cove from San Antonio, and visited about a dozen churches before we found the church we knew God called us to: Trinity Worship Center, or TWC. It was our second Sunday there, and we had a guest minister who flowed in a prophetic anointing. After preaching, this man came straight to Matt and told him, "You are called into the ministry and you've been running from God. He's going to send you into the desert for a time to prepare you for ministry." Wow! We were in tears. We both figured he meant a figurative desert, you know, a dry place. About three months later, Matt was sent to Bosnia for six months. Maybe this was the "desert" God spoke of? Nope. Two years later, when our son was nine months old, Matt came up on orders to go to the literal Sinai Desert for one year. Amazing! This was the desert that Moses went through. We put all our stuff in storage, he shipped out, and I flew up north to live with my mother-in-law. This was one of the roughest years of my life. My husband was in the desert preparing for ministry. Meanwhile, I was living in a place that was cold and wet with a baby and a woman I didn't know very well. People in Texas are very friendly. People in Seattle are not as friendly, at all. It was a very trying season.

I joined an athletic club nearby and I went every day. At that time, my mile time had increased because of the birth of my son. So, I figured I would work on lowering my time. I had a whole year to get faster. After about eight months, I was back on track, running three miles in less than thirty-five minutes. I had made friends with a personal trainer and was telling her of my accomplishment. That's when a nearby trainer piped in. "Hey! Do you love to run? Come run with my club!"

I was pretty intimidated by a running club, so I said, "No, thanks." However, he continued to hound me every time he saw me in the club. "Come run with us!" Every. Single. Time.

Runners love to run and they want others to enjoy running like they do. They don't care how fast you can run or how far you can run. They don't care what shoes you wear, although they want you to have good shoes so you don't get injured. They just love to run and they want you to come run with them. If you have truly been set free from the power of the devil, then you want *everyone* to experience freedom the same way you have.

When I was thirteen, I hung out with a bunch of juvenile delinquents, literally. The year before, during my seventh-grade year, I had attended three different schools (the last one being in a completely different state). I started eighth grade in yet another school. Let me tell you, thirteen is not the age you want to be starting a new school. It was rough. I can remember several lunches eating alone in the bathroom and crying because I didn't have any friends. I eventually made friends with the only kids who accepted me—the "stoners," or "heads" as they were called. I wasn't a jock. I quit band. I wasn't rich; in fact, I wasn't even middle class. I wasn't a cheerleader. I wasn't "new wave." I was poor, white, and a fan of rock music. I fit in with the stoners. Since I had already dabbled in smoking pot and had tried alcohol, it was an easy fit. I became a stoner. Most of the kids I hung out with lived in the neighborhood just down the street from my apartment complex. We would hang out and get stoned. A lot of these kids had juvenile records for theft and other minor offenses and were known and watched by the police. Therefore, I became known and watched by the police.

> "Do not be so deceived *and* misled! Evil companionships (communion, associations) corrupt *and* deprave good manners *and* morals *and* character" **1 Corinthians 15:33**.

This one time, a friend asked if she could spend the night with me. The next morning the police showed up at my home banging on the door. I was terrified. What had they come for? Was I getting arrested? I had pot under my bed for goodness sake! I looked out my back window and another officer was in the back, in case anyone tried to run away.

I opened the door.

"Is Michelle here?" the officer asked.

"No." I lied.

"Could you please step outside, Crystal?" the officer stated.

He knew my name. I was terrified. I stepped outside and the officer grabbed me and handcuffed me.

"You are under arrest for harboring a runaway," he said.

"What?" I yelled through tears.

I was crying so hard I couldn't breathe. The officer threw me and my friend in the back of his cruiser and took us down to the station to book us. I was thirteen and going to jail for harboring a runaway. I had broken the law in other ways prior to this, but had gotten away with it. Not this time. I cried in terror the whole way down to the station. I don't think I've ever been so afraid. Both officers began to lecture me on my life, on where it was heading: Down the wrong path. They knew me. They had been watching me and following me. I was arrested in the early morning and ended up spending the entire day in a jail cell. Not a cell for children, a holding cell for adults. It smelled like feces, urine, and vomit. There was obscene writing on the walls. It was dirty, smelly, and I was scared. I knew I never wanted to go back. The officers released me to my mother at about nine that night. They had tried reaching her all day, but she couldn't be found. Now, maybe they were trying to scare me or teach me a lesson, and that was really just a drill, an illegal drill quite possibly. They went old school, "scared straight" on me and it worked.

After that, I tried influencing my stoner friends to stop all illegal activity, but it didn't work. So, I stopped hanging out with them. The next year I was sent back to New Mexico to live with some old friends to a small town called Ruidoso, away from my Mom. But when I returned to San Antonio the following year, I found a whole new group of kids to hang out with. There was no way I was going to live a life in and out of jail. No way.

"So if the Son liberates you [makes you free men], then you are really *and* unquestionably free" **John 8:36.**

If you have been set free from your prison of bondage, then you should not want to return and you should want to set others free! Jesus came to destroy all the works of the devil in your life, therefore giving you freedom.

"[But] he who commits sin [who practices evildoing] is of the devil [takes his character from the evil one], for the devil has sinned (violated the divine law) from the beginning. The reason the Son of God was made manifest (visible) was to undo (destroy, loosen, and dissolve) the works the devil [has done]" **1 John 3:8.**

Have you experienced his freedom? If so, you should run to help others escape their prison. A free person loves being free and wants to help others experience freedom. Freedom is the reason so many people put their lives on the line to abolish slavery. There is nothing like freedom. You were in prison! You were in your sin and you could not escape. He made you free. Do you grasp the reality of what He did on the cross? He didn't just cover your sin: He set you free from sin. He set you free from all fear.

"For [the Spirit which] you have now received [is] not a spirit of slavery to put you once more in bondage to fear, but you have received the Spirit of adoption [the Spirit producing sonship] in [the bliss of] which we cry, Abba (Father)! Father" **Romans 8:15.**

"And also that He might deliver *and* completely set free all those who through the [haunting] fear of death were held in bondage throughout the whole course of their lives" **Hebrews 2:15.**

You are free! You have an obligation now to go and set others free. Go and share with the others the freedom that they can have in Jesus. Don't you want to keep others out of that nasty, dirty, smelly, cold, scary jail cell?

"[Strive to] save others, snatching [them] out of [the] fire; on others take pity [but] with fear, loathing even the garment spotted by the flesh *and* polluted by their sensuality" **Jude 23.**

Again, I ask you, have you been set free? Then, snatch people out of their prison of hopelessness and despair. You have the God-appointed task of setting people free. Yes, you. God has placed the people in your life for a reason. He wants you to help set them free. Put your life on the line to set the captives free! Doesn't that sound exciting and fulfilling?

Chapter 17

Never, Never, Never Quit

Have you ever failed? Or maybe a better question would be: how many times have you failed? Don't think about it too long, for it might get you down. I have failed, but I've never quit. There is no prize for quitting.

I mentioned that walking to a runner is failing. A runner runs, she doesn't walk. Well, I have walked more times than I can count. I have failed time and time again. Especially in the early days of my running; I had to walk a lot. I think I probably walked more than I ran. Even now, after running for twenty years, I still have to walk. I have bad days where I am just plum tuckered out, or my feet hurt and I need to walk. I still fail, time and time again. There's generally a good reason, or rather excuse, as to why I fail on any particular run. I ate too much and my stomach hurts. My legs are tight because I didn't stretch. I just flat ran out of energy. Whatever the case may be, I have failed. But, I don't quit running. The next day, I get up, pray, read my Bible, and go for my run. This day I will finish! That's what I tell myself. That is the brilliance of a new day—it brings a new start and new mercy.

"It is because of the Lord's mercy *and* loving-kindness that we are not consumed, because His [tender] compassions fail not. They are new every morning; great *and* abundant is Your stability *and* faithfulness" **Lamentations 3:22-23.**

I fail. I have failed Him, myself, my family, my husband, my children, my friends, and the list goes on and on. I have failed and I will fail. But, that does *not* make me a failure. It does not define me. His mercy is new every day.

There is a Phillips, Craig, and Dean song titled "Mercy Came Running." Ever hear of it? Here is a paraphrase of the lyrics: "Mercy comes running to me, past my failures, past my pain and disappointments, past my sin and shame; Mercy continues to pursue me."

Have you failed? Mercy runs! He gives you new mercy every day. Get up! Don't wallow in your failings. You are not a failure! His mercy is new. His mercy pursues you. His mercy runs to you, picks you up, puts you back on your feet, and says, "Get out there and run! You can do this. I will go with you. I will not fail you."

Forget about yesterday—it's gone. You cannot go back and make it up. Leave it alone. His mercy for yesterday is gone. He's giving you mercy for today. Did you walk instead of run yesterday? Maybe you didn't even get out of bed. leave it be! His mercy is for today.

"I do not consider, brethren, that I have captured *and* made it my own [yet]; but one thing I do [it is my one aspiration]: forgetting what lies behind and straining forward to what lies ahead, I press on toward the goal to win the [supreme and heavenly] prize to which God in Christ Jesus is calling us upward. So let those [of us] who are spiritually mature *and* full-grown have this mind *and* hold these convictions; and if in any respect you have a different attitude of mind, God will make that clear to you also" **Philippians 3:13-15.**

Coach Pete Carroll says this: "*It's not how you start; it's how you finish.*" Man, the Seahawks have a way of keeping you on the edge of your seat. They are so slow to start. But, somewhere in that third and fourth quarter, there comes the boom! They turn it up!

Maybe you're a slow starter, it doesn't matter. IT ONLY MATTERS HOW YOU FINISH! Churchill said this: "*Never, never, never quit.*" Quitting is not an option. Get up, dust yourself off, and move on. How do you think one of the winning-est coaches in history felt about quitting? Here is a list of Vince Lombardi Quotes:

"The difference between a successful person and others is not a lack of strength, not a lack of knowledge, but rather a lack in will."

"Once you learn to quit, it becomes a habit."

"Winning isn't everythingbut wanting to win is."

"The greatest accomplishment is not in never falling, but in rising again after you fall."

"It's not whether you got knocked down; it's whether you get back up."

"The real glory is being knocked to your knees and then coming back. That's real glory. That's the essence of it."

"I firmly believe that any man's finest hour, the greatest fulfillment of all that he holds dear, is that moment when he has worked his heart out in a good cause and lies exhausted on the field of battlevictorious."

"The man on top of the mountain didn't fall there."

"Winners never quit and quitters never win."

Up here in the Pacific Northwest we have some pretty cold days. Matt and I will run on the trail in thirty-degree, weather no problem. Heck, sometimes it'll be twenty-four degrees, and, in that kind of wintery weather, it takes a mile to a mile and a half to warm up, even in cold-weather running gear. But, once you get going, you build up a good sweat and can get fairly hot. However, if you stop and walk and let your body cool down, the sweat gets cold fast, cooling down your body and making you colder than when you first started.

About a year ago, God gave me a dream of a deer climbing up a snowy embankment. The deer would get half way up and slide down, then a lion would come out at the base of the hill and scratch the deer. The scratch was small at first, but the more times the deer went up the embankment and slid down, the deeper the scratch from the lion became. This happened several times, until the deer grew exhausted and finally gave up. That's when other lions came in and tore apart the deer. I prayed on this dream for a few days and God revealed it to me in the book of Jeremiah.

"But these have altogether broken the yoke
And burst the bonds.
Therefore a lion from the forest shall slay them,
A wolf of the deserts shall destroy them;
A leopard will watch over their cities.
Everyone who goes out from there
  shall be torn in pieces,
Because their transgressions are many;
Their backslidings have increased"
Jeremiah 5:6.

God revealed to me that there are severe consequences for persistent backsliding. It is absolutely spiritual. Every time you backslide (fall away from God and back into your sinful ways), you get scratched by Satan. You open yourself up to spiritual attacks from the enemy. You are no longer under God's protective care. But also, the more you backslide, the more difficult coming back to God becomes. Jesus talked about this very thing:

> "When an unclean spirit goes out of a man, he goes through dry places, seeking rest, and finds none. 44 Then he says, 'I will return to my house from which I came.' And when he comes, he finds it empty, swept, and put in order.45 Then he goes and takes with him seven other spirits more wicked than himself, and they enter and dwell there; and the last *state* of that man is worse than the first" **Matthew 12:43-45.**

When you quit running with God and fall back into your old sinful self, Satan enters. Do this frequently enough and Satan will start bringing some ugly dudes with him. That's when you find yourself in a worse state than before you had Christ. Say for example, you were an alcoholic before Christ and He redeemed you and cleaned you up. You endure for a time, but revert back to alcohol when times get hard. The next time you try to come back to God, that alcohol bondage is much stronger than it had been the first time around. There is a spiritual battle going on for your soul. Don't quit. Don't return to your vomit.

> "As a dog returns to his own vomit,
> *So* a fool repeats his folly" **Proverbs 26:11.**

God's mercy is greater than your failures. If you fall, he will pick you up. Every single time! But, if you return to your old life of sin, you trample on the blood of Christ and put yourself in a very precarious situation.

Don't quit this race. It's all worth it in the end. He's worth it. You're worth it. Keep moving. Don't go back. There is nothing for you in that old life of sin. That old man that you were is dead and buried. Don't resurrect him. If you need help, cry out to Him and He will come running.

Like I mentioned earlier, there is no prize for quitting. I knew a family that threw a graduation party for their daughter despite the fact that she had quit high school just prior to graduation. Heck, I didn't even get a graduation party and I graduated high school—with honors. How do you rectify that in your mind? You do not get a diploma for completing "most" of your high school requirements, or for "trying" your hardest, but not finishing. Likewise, you do not (or should not) get a retirement party for quitting your job. You get a retirement party after you have loyally worked for a company for years. There is no prize for the quitter. Now, maybe you struggled with high school and quit because you were having a lot of trouble in classes and emotional issues, but then got your GED. Good for you! You went back to pick up where you left off and finished the course. You had to walk for a while, but you got back in there and ran through the finish line. Well done.

Both my kids ran track and both competed in the hurdles. My kids got some long legs! I've been to a lot of track meets and I here to tell you that the kids that get the most cheers are the ones who trip and fall but get right back up to finish the race. They may not win, but they do not quit. With pain on their face and blood on their knees, they finish the race that has been set before them. A few years ago, there was a video going around of a 600-meter race where the girl took a nasty head plant into the track. She got up and got back in there–and actually won her race! It was amazing and inspiring. See, you will all fail at some time in this race. Sometimes others will even knock you down. Sometimes you just won't be able to jump high enough to get over that hurdle and you will fall. You have to get back up and keep going! You cannot quit your race!

Chapter 18

All in or Nothing at All

Have I convinced you yet to head out and buy some sneakers and hit the pavement running? "Not quite, but good try, Crystal!" I know, I know. Running is not for everyone and when you first start out it is not easy. Running, however, gets easier the more you run. And the more you run, the easier it gets! You cannot however, do a Stairmaster and think that it will improve your running. The only way to improve on your running is to run. Period. It's kind of the same thing with pushups.

I remember when I met my husband, I could run for sure, but I could only do about five pushups, and those weren't even "to the standard," as Matt liked to say. He told me, "Crystal, if you want to get better at pushups, you have to do pushups." You can do some weight training to strengthen your chest muscles, but in the end, you have to do pushups. I didn't want to do pushups. Pushups aren't fun, but I had made myself a goal to do twenty pushups "to the standard," and so I began. It wasn't easy, but over the course of three months, starting with my five pushups and building upon that, I worked up to doing thirty "to the standard" pushups. I put in the effort every day to be able to hit this goal.

Dear beginning runner, the more you run, the easier it gets.

You learn how to have good foot placement and good form. Your breathing becomes uniform and relaxed. You learn about your body, about what stride works best for you. There are absolutes to running, like I mentioned in Chapter X, "Have Good Form." Chest out, head up, and shoulders back to open up your airways and make it easier for you to breath—that's a big part of it. And this is true for everyone. We all need the same good form to run effectively. When it comes to stride, there are many varying opinions and options. I read an article by one doctor that stated the best stride was a shorter one with increased speed. He said that this stride was the easiest on your knees. Well, I tried it. I have long legs. I'm 5' 11" and my husband is 6' 5", and we have the same inseam if that tells you anything. The shorter stride didn't work for me. I prefer a long stride, kind of like I am walking on the moon. It is what I have always done and I have never had any shin splints or knee problems. Again, good form is absolute and universal, but the stride you choose when running is subjective and personal.

However, the call of Christ is not subjective. It is an absolute all or nothing. You cannot be a part-time Christian, and you cannot be a half-way Christian. God is not interested in part of you sometimes or half of you all the time. He wants all of you all the time. This walk is an all-in, all-of-you, all-the-time walk. When you surrendered to Jesus and made Him your Lord and Savior, your life was forfeited. Your ways, your thoughts, your plans have all been surrendered to Jesus. This is what it means to take up your cross and follow Him.

> "And He said to all, If any person wills to come after
> Me, let him deny himself [disown himself, forget,
> lose sight of himself and his own interests, refuse

and give up himself] and take up his cross daily and follow Me [cleave steadfastly to Me, conform wholly to My example in living and, if need be, in dying also]" **Luke 9:23.**

The call of Jesus is daily. It doesn't matter if you served Him yesterday, He wants you today. It is a choice we all have to make every morning when we step out of bed. "Today, I am going to seek Him and serve Him." That's waking up and getting into good form daily. Now, the way in which you serve him is your stride. It can be long and slow, or short and fast, or maybe a little in between. The way in which you serve the Lord is not going to look like the way in which I serve Him. We are not all called to serve Him the same. You are a part of a whole body of moving, serving, working parts. Your stride should look different than my stride.

My husband and I were out running last week when he asked me, "Honey, how many days do you have to run a week to be considered a runner?" I replied, "I think you should run most days of the week to be considered a true runner. Therefore, at least four, but five or six is optimum." I mean, how can you be considered a runner unless you run more often than you don't? Myself, I run at least five days a week and occasionally sneak in that sixth day when possible. I would run all seven days, except that I know my body needs a rest.

For the Christ follower, how many days do you have to follow Christ to be considered a follower? Shouldn't the answer be every single day? Jesus said, "Take up your cross daily." How can you get up and say, "I think I'll take off Tuesdays from following Christ." This is, of course, ridiculous. But in essence it's how a lot of people take their relationship with the Lord. If you are married, would you take a day off from your marriage to just go and do whatever it is you wanted to do, considering yourself a single person again? I hope not. That's a good way to not stay married for starters. But, this is how people treat Christ. Maybe not consciously, but when you choose your path over His, this is what you are saying to Jesus.

> "Do you not know that your body is the temple (the very sanctuary) of the Holy Spirit Who lives within you, Whom you have received [as a Gift] from God? You are not your own, You were bought with a price [purchased with a preciousness and paid for, made His own]. So then, honor God *and* bring glory to Him in your body" **1 Corinthians 6:19-20.**

When you gave yourself to Him at the altar, you gave Him every day of your life. You gave Him your ways, your plans, your thoughts, your words. Yes, your words. He cares how you live, how you dress, how you think, how you walk and how you talk. He wants all of you!

Did you know that you are irreplaceable? When I was around the age of eighteen, I had a boyfriend that broke up with me after several months of dating. I had a friend that overheard him talking to his friends, who said, "You can do so much better than Crystal. She is totally replaceable." Now as mad as I was, that hurt me just as much. Maybe my friend shouldn't have told me about it, but he thought he was helping me and being a good friend. Those words stung and I carried them around with me for a long time. However, after I came to the Lord, He began speaking life into me. He began telling me that there was no one like me. I was not replaceable. But He said something interesting, too. God said people *could* discard me, but not because I wasn't worthy, because of their own problems and insecurities. He spoke this so much into my life that I walked in confidence when I met Matt. I walked believing that I was worthy of his love. I was ready to be his wife. I was irreplaceable, a woman of great value.

"[Inasmuch as we] refute arguments *and* theories *and* reasonings and every proud *and* lofty thing that sets itself up against the [true] knowledge of God; and we lead every thought *and* purpose away captive into the obedience of Christ (the Messiah, the Anointed One)" **2 Corinthians 10:5.**

A runner knows her worth and takes those lies of the enemy captive. She knows that she is irreplaceable. Your mind needs to belong to the Lord if you are going to run your race strong. You have to run with confidence or you will trip and fall.

"But I tell you, on the day of judgment men will have to give account for every idle (inoperative, nonworking) word they speak" **Matthew 12:36.**

This scripture in Matthew should give us comfort in knowing that God will take care of those who speak against us, but it should also be a warning for us to think before we speak. Every thought, purpose, and word belongs to Him. Do you find this challenging? I know I do! It's not easy and it's not simple. Some days are a hard-fought bloody battle until my head hits the pillow at night. But, He is with you! He helps you! He strengthens you! He forgives when you mess up. All He asks is for you to surrender. Just put your hands up and surrender it all to him. Let go and see how wonderful he is to supply your every need.

What is keeping you from giving him all of you? trust? Fear? Let it go. He is faithful.

> "So let us seize *and* hold fast *and* retain without wavering the hope we cherish *and* confess *and* our acknowledgement of it, for He Who promised is reliable (sure) *and* faithful to His word" **Hebrews 10:23.**

A huge deterrence to being "all in" is shame and guilt. These two silent killers will keep you from giving Him your *all.* I carried around guilt from a childhood of sexual abuse because I thought it was my fault. I know it's ridiculous that a nine-year-old would cause a twenty-three-year-old man to molest her, but I thought that, and so I carried that guilt. It wasn't until my daughter turned nine years old that I became aware of the shame I was carrying around for a sin that wasn't mine. I literally remember the moment this happened. We were driving along, singing to some Christian music, when the Lord spoke to me.

"Crystal," His voice whispered.

"Here I am, Lord," I replied.

"Look at your daughter," He said.

"Yes, she is beautiful," I replied.

"She is nine," He said.

"Yes, Lord," I replied.

"That was the age you were when you were molested," He said.

I looked at my baby girl, my little "mini me," and I cried. She was so sweet and so innocent.

"So were you, Crystal," the Lord said. "Let go of the guilt. Let go of the shame."

Can you hear the Master's words? Let it go. Let go of the guilt.

Let go of the shame. Give it over to Him. He can handle it. He will take it from you. He will cleanse your hurting heart and fill that void so then you can give Him truly your all and be all in. Run hard in your lane!

Chapter 19

A Dog is Still a Dog

Ranger is a pretty cool dog, as far as dogs are concerned. He's mostly well behaved and he obeys us the majority of the time. He's playful and great with kids, and he'd be a terrific running partner if it weren't for the fact that he likes to stop and pee on everything.

I do not like to stop when I am running, nor do I want to have to slow down so my dog can pee. He doesn't need to pee, he just wants to mark his territory—at least a dozen times on any given run. It doesn't matter if he peed there yesterday, he's peeing in the same spot again today. It drives me crazy! I've tried everything to get him to stop, but nothing works. He determined to mark his place, even if it means stopping in the middle of the road to go. And even though he's a male dog, he'll even pee like a girl if he has to in order to mark his territory (see: middle of the road). He doesn't care whether I get mad and yell. Matt just laughs at us. "Crystal, he's a dog." Matt's right. A dog will do what a dog does—because he's a dog and nothing I do will change him. or his nature. Which is to mark his territory. It's in him to do that. He's a dog.

> "Can the Ethiopian change his skin or the leopard its spots? *Then* may you also do good who are accustomed to do evil" **Jeremiah 13:23.**

If you live in this world, you will have to deal with people. Contrary to popular belief, people are not inherently good nor do they automatically have "good hearts."

> "The heart *is* deceitful above all *things,* And desperately wicked; Who can know it?" **Jeremiah 17:9.**

I know you'd like to believe that everyone is good, kind and loving, but it's just not true. People are people and they do what they were born to do. You cannot change your own nature, and most certainly cannot change someone else's nature. Why do you get all shook up and surprised when others treat you poorly? A dog is gonna do what a dog does.

Now, as far as dogs go, I have never met a lab I didn't like. Have you ever read the headline: "Lab attacks kid!"? Probably not. By nature, labs are gentle and have a good temperament. They make great family dogs. Yet, not all dogs are like the lab. Did you know that the dog who bites the most is the Chihuahua? You just don't hear about it as often because they are such little dogs and they can't do much damage. The nature of the Chihuahua is to bite. Why? Maybe they have a Napoleon Complex, I don't know. Because of this they don't always make good family dogs. For that matter neither do Dalmatians, because they are prone to biting and are easily excitable. It is in their nature. Where am I going with this? Such as it is with people. Some are labs and some are Chihuahuas and there is every kind of person with every kind of nature in between. Some people are going to just lash out and bite you and others, like the lab, will just go and sit in their corner and sulk if they're upset.

You have to learn how to love people, anyway. You have to love them if they bite you or if they sit and sulk. You have to learn how to love the people around you even if they are messing up your run because they keep stopping to pee on everything.

Matt and I have been fulltime pastors since 2003, and boy, have some people peed all over us and our ministry! It would be shameful for me to elaborate, but let's just say we've been called every name in the book, we've been gossiped about, falsely accused, defamed; our kids have been attacked we've been called false teachers and wolves in sheep clothing; we've been accused of being unloving, unforgiving, and the list goes on and on.

How do we keep going? Well, people are people. Just because they are in church doesn't mean they know the Lord and even if they are born again, doesn't mean their mind has been renewed or that they are even listening and obeying the Holy Spirit. It has been my experience that people do what they want to do, and they don't really care how it affects others. And besides this, another hard fact is the people that you love on the most and help out the most, will hurt you the greatest. Remember Judas? He betrayed Jesus with a kiss. Judas, Jesus's close friend, his inner circle guy betrayed Jesus more than anyone. Judas was one of the original twelve to walk and live with Jesus for His three years of ministry. If Jesus isn't above being hurt and betrayed, then how can we not expect to be?

Here's the thing, you cannot let biting and betrayal, or even small interruptions (like pee breaks) to affect you. I'm still running, even if I have to drag my dog while he's peeing. I'm not stopping. You have to love, forgive, and keep going on. I hear way too many stories of people that have stopped going to church because "they were mean to me." Seriously? Get over it. This person did this, that person did that, this person isn't doing what they're supposed to be doing, and that person looked at me the wrong way, and yada, yada, yada. How are you going to let a dog keep you from doing what you know you should be doing before God? It is the dog's nature to pee on everything! Take it to the Lord, lay it on the altar, and let go! Has someone hurt you? Love them anyway. Has someone said something mean? Pray for them anyway.

> "But I say to you, love your enemies, bless those who curse you, do good to those who hate you, and pray for those who spitefully use you and persecute you"
> **Matthew 5:44.**

My husband and I joke about this quite often. And so I pose this question to you again: What if the pastors just decided they weren't coming back to church because they were offended? What if you showed up to church on Sunday and the pastor was just gone? He decided he had enough of people, of someone hurt his feelings, and he just stayed home. I don't know one pastor that has done that. They can't. The pastor has to show up to teach and preach the Word. He is the leader, and without the pastor it is the blind leading the blind. But, this is what people do all the time. They get offended and leave church. We are forced to work things out. It is our church, we planted it, and it is our baby. We are not leaving because someone was mean to us. We are not leaving because we don't like someone else's behavior. The church is full of broken, hurting people and sometimes you are going to get hurt. That doesn't mean you need to move on. Don't leave! God has ordained for you to be in a local body and has placed ministry leaders over you for your benefit!

I'm truly sorry if you have been hurt, and I cannot promise you that you will not be hurt again, but the church needs you. We work together in the Body for His purposes. Let go of the pain. Forgive. Love. Pray for the Body. Pray for your church, her pastors and her people. Work hard at not being so thin-skinned. Remember—when someone hurts you, it's just their human nature coming out. Pray for eyes that see how He sees, and a heart to love how He loves. He will help you overcome hurt, pain, and offenses. Jesus even tells us that "Offenses will come"; there will be times we will be resented, disregarded and insulted, and these offenses are occasions for us to fall into sin So, what is the remedy for an offense? Forgiveness.

> "Then He said to the disciples, 'It is impossible that no offenses should come, but woe to him through whom they do come! It would be better for him if a millstone were hung around his neck, and he were thrown into the sea, than that he should offend one of these little ones. Take heed to yourselves. If your brother sins against you, rebuke him; and if he repents, forgive him. And if he sins against you seven times in a day, and seven times in a day returns to you, saying, 'I repent,' you shall forgive him'" **Luke 17:1-4.**

Is forgiveness always easy? No. Just ask me. I asked Matt a few years ago what he thought my greatest weakness was. Yes, this is me. Constantly examining myself, every day crucifying this nasty flesh. (The struggle is real.) He said, "You let others steal your joy."

Wanting clarification, I followed up with, "Do I hold a grudge?"

"No, you just hold onto hurt way too long and let it affect you." Hmmm, I had to think about this for a moment. It was true. I held onto hurt way far too long. I allowed hurtful events to hurt me again and again, robbing me of joy. Robbing me of peace. Since that conversation, I am learning to let go and forgive. I'm not there yet, but I am getting better. Don't let others steal your joy and rob you of your peace. Besides all this, He will handle the offender. Let Him defend you. You perform for an audience of One. Work on pleasing God *alone*. Did I happen to mention that this race is chock full of obstacles and difficulties? "Here I am on mile 116 of this race and there's a stumbling block of offense up ahead in thirty feet." Well, here we go again, just when I thought no more obstacles would be on my run! Yet, you cannot run away from difficulties. To run around this upcoming one, only means there will be another a few more miles down the road. It doesn't matter if you are on mile three, or mile 333, and it doesn't matter how smooth the run has been up to this point. There will be offenses that you need to learn to navigate through the power of forgiveness.

Chapter 20

Running with
a Bad Back

Does someone you know have chronic pain? Do you? I have suffered and dealt with anxiety and depression most of my life. I also have body aches and joint pain from an auto accident back in 1997. My husband Matt has chronic back pain since his days in the military. Most days the pain ranges from a three to an eight for him, and on occasion it will shoot up to a ten. When this happens, he's out of commission for sometimes as much as two weeks. He gets disability from the military and sees a PT on a regular basis.

Fortunately for me, he hasn't been told he can't run. (This is sometimes unfortunate for him.) Sometimes running can exasperate a bad back, but not in his case. As long as he keeps good form (see Chapter 14). In fact, his doctor gave him several exercises to increase his back strength—and not just stretching, actual weight-bearing exercises. He also told Matt something profound:

> "There are two types of people with chronic pain. The first one lets his pain run his life. His pain dictates his day, what he will or will not do. The second type runs his life in spite of the pain. He does what he wants, when he wants, regardless of the pain. In all my years, the first type al-

ways gets worse and the person becomes more negative. The second type of person gets better and their outlook more positive over time."

Which are you? You're going to have to be honest with yourself to answer this question.

I'm not trying to minimize your pain, please hear my heart. I also realize that my pain is not your pain, and we all experience pain differently and cope with it differently. But I ask you, does your pain run your life? Or are you going to run regardless of your pain?

Pain is not just physical. I think maybe I'd prefer physical pain over emotional pain. Because of my life experiences, my emotional pain stunted my growth in the Lord—I was circling the same mountain. "I can't do that, it's too painful." I didn't think it was possible to overcome the emotional pain from my past. It's interesting to me that the OT law gave people thirty days to mourn the death of someone—emotional pain.

> "And the children of Israel wept for Moses in the plains of Moab thirty days. So the days of weeping *and* mourning for Moses ended" **Deuteronomy 34:8.**

> "She shall put off the clothes of her captivity, remain in your house, and mourn her father and her mother a full month; after that you may go in to her and be her husband, and she shall be your wife" **Deuteronomy 21:13.**

> "Now when all the congregation saw that Aaron was dead, all the house of Israel mourned for Aaron thirty days" **Numbers 20:29.**

God gave Israel a month to mourn, and then they were told to move on. Now, let's not be legalistic about the law, but rather look at the spirit of the law. God gave His people a certain amount of time to mourn and then they needed to get on with their life. *This is for you today.* How long will you mourn your pain and loss? I had severe emotional pain, deep scars, but the Lord asked me, "Crystal, do you want to be healed? Then, you have to stop grieving over what was done to you and let me heal you." God is speaking to you right now. It's time to stop mourning and get running. If you stay in the circling pattern of mourning, you will never run the race God has set before you. Pain can cause you to become stagnant.

You were never meant to mourn your whole life. I don't know your story and I don't know your pain, but you have to get running again. If you let your pain control your life, you will only get worse and worse. This Scripture speaks of the mind (heart, will, emotions) controlling the man:

> "The upright (honorable, intrinsically good) man out of the good treasure [stored] in his heart produces what is upright (honorable and intrinsically good), and the evil man out of the evil storehouse brings forth that which is depraved (wicked and intrinsically evil); for out of the abundance (overflow) of the heart his mouth speaks" **Luke 6:45.**

Mourn, yes. But after mourning, it's time to live again. Repent. Change your mind. Cast out the wrong thoughts. Change your words. Speak life-giving, positive words over your pain! I know it hurts. I know it's painful. But, you were not created to live in mourning. You were not created to just survive. You were created to soar. You were created to run.

One of the most painful experiences for me happened early on in our ministry. There was a young man who was saved at our church and shortly after, he was diagnosed with cancer and given six weeks to live. Our church rallied around him, praying for a miracle, believing God would grant one. Through his suffering, his dad came to know the Lord and walked with his son through the pain. At the end of six weeks, he died. I was at the hospital with the family when he passed into the arms of Jesus. I held the hand of this nineteen-year-old's dad, while he stood by helplessly watching his son die. Then afterwards, it was the most painful thing I had ever experienced—watching this man break down in the corner of the hospital room after losing his only son. It wasn't my grief, but I felt his grief and his pain. And I felt completely helpless. It was overwhelming.

I watched him over the next year. He kept coming to church and he kept working and running his race. He didn't allow the pain to keep him from finishing, and I was able to see with my own eyes how God brought restoration into his life with a new wife and son.

> "For His anger is but for a moment, but His favor is for a lifetime *or* in His favor is life. Weeping may endure for a night, but joy comes in the morning"
> **Psalm 30:5.**

Joy comes when you stop mourning and run. Run through the pain. It *will* get easier and better.

My grandma had rheumatoid arthritis, RA, as I mentioned in the opening. It was very severe. Her doctor's orders were to exercise and move her joints *through the pain.* I spoke extensively to the doctor about this and she assured me time and again that the more my grandmother exercised, the easier it would be and the less pain she would have. "However, those first few weeks are going to be hell," she warned. She would have horrible pain, but she would need to work *through the pain*. So, every night, I brought out the exercise bike, set my grandmother in a make-shift chair (so she could use it as a recumbent bike), and I made her pedal. She hated it. She wanted to stop after less than five minutes. I made her continue. I reassured her that the exercise would not kill her and that after a short while, she *would* feel better. Eventually, she did. She even worked up to being able to get into the pool and do water aerobics. She worked *through the pain* to get to the victory on the other side.

> "Looking away [from all that will distract] to Jesus, Who is the Leader *and* the Source of our faith [giving the first incentive for our belief] and is also its Finisher [bringing it to maturity and perfection]. He, for the joy [of obtaining the prize] that was set before Him, endured the cross, despising *and* ignoring the shame, and is now seated at the right hand of the throne of God" **Hebrews 12:2.**

Like Jesus, you can endure the pain in order to get to the victory on the other side. But, you have to go through it! There is no going around and there is definitely no camping in your pain. Surround yourself with positive people that will make you pedal your bike.

Like I said earlier, I have dealt with anxiety and depression for most of my life. There was a period of about six years where it was really bad. I had horrible panic attacks and chest pain. I wanted to ball up in a fetal position and cut off everyone and everything. But God said, "Keep running. I will go with you through the furnace." These were rough years. I had two small children, Matt worked sixty hours a week at a "normal" job and we had just planted the church. I had to keep running. I couldn't stop. I couldn't retreat. It was painful. I was tired, weary, and worn out. I was alone and depressed. I didn't sleep and barely ate, but I kept running. At no time did God tell me to stop, and He certainly hadn't healed me. "Go through the pain, Crystal."

I asked Him once after years of going through the fiery furnace why my pain was hanging on for so long.

He answered, "I am teaching you compassion."

Ouch! I cried and complained a little, but quickly came to my senses as I surrendered and cried out, "Lord, mold me and shape me for Your purpose. Use this pain to bring forth good fruit and character." This is what I prayed.

I knew it was true. I desperately loved people, but because of my upbringing, I lived in survival mode. My attitude was always, "Get over it, Crystal, and move on." That was the attitude I felt others should have, too. I didn't have a lot of compassion, so God had to instill compassion in me through suffering.

What is He teaching you through the pain? Maybe you're living in it a little longer than expected because He is perfecting your character? Don't be stubborn. Let the Master Potter mold you. Let Him shape you. He is making you into a vessel for His purpose. Don't buckle under His hands. Keep running through the pain. It will get better!

Chapter 21

Sometimes
You Fall

Notice I said "fall" not "fail."

Funny story. One morning, Matt and I took Ranger out for a run on our favorite trail. It was about thirty-eight degrees, a little crisp for my tastes, but a runner runs no matter what the weather. Now, I have said before that Ranger is a pretty good running partner, but he's not great. He's a great running partner in the sense that he is always willing to run with me and keep me company. He likes to pee on everything, as I have stated in another chapter and he also likes to check out other dogs on occasion—not every dog, just certain dogs, and you can never be sure as to which dogs attract his attention. The trail we run on is about three feet wide and we always stay as far right as we can go, knowing Ranger likes other dogs. However, most other people with dogs do not give us the same courtesy. They will walk down the middle with their dog, not even controlling what the dog does. This one day in particular, there was a lady coming toward us walking two` dogs on a double leash. She was around sixty and petite, and these dogs were too much for her to handle, so I figured we'd better manage ours.

So, Matt and I are running, like we do, and I call out "Dog

ahead" so Matt knows to pull Ranger closer to him and all the way to the right of the trail. Well, Ranger caught eyes with one of the other dogs anyway. He ran forward—in front of me—and pulled hard to the left. I tripped and fell over him, landing hard on my left side, scraping my knee and hip, bruising my shoulder and elbow. Matt then trips over me landing hard on his right side. Ranger stops and stares at us lying on the ground as if to stay, "What the heck are y'all doing lying on the ground?" The lady stops and turns and asks if we're okay. We get up fast and continue to walk as best as we can (hobbling was more like it), completely red-faced and embarrassed. Then we both start laughing uncontrollably at how we must have looked to that lady. "We just made her day!" Matt said and laughed.

This is life, my friend. Sometimes you fall. There is no reason or rhyme, you just fall. Someone you love dies. You lose a job. You lose a friendship. Your home catches fire. Your car breaks down. That's life. It is a series of mountains and valleys. In a day, Job lost everything. Everything! In. A. Day. But, it didn't stop him from continuing to seek and worship the Lord.

> "Then Job arose and rent his robe and shaved his head and fell down upon the ground and worshiped And said, Naked (without possessions) came I [into this world] from my mother's womb, and naked (without possessions) shall I depart. The Lord gave and the Lord has taken away; blessed (praised and magnified in worship) be the name of the Lord"
> Job 1:20-21.

When I came to the Lord at twenty-three, I had nothing. If I wasn't clear on this before, I mean nothing. The year before I had committed adultery and was living with that man in Charlotte,

NC. I was a mess. My blood pressure was stroke-level high because my ex was stalking me and threatening to kill me, and I had severe panic attacks and depression because of it. I was always looking over my shoulder at every turn. I was drinking a lot of alcohol to numb my pain. I was in a very bad place.

My mom had recently been saved and she began praying for me. She came to visit me and just wanted to pray for me. She kept encouraging me to go to church, but I didn't want to meet God in the condition I was in. I was scared. I was alone. I felt dirty. No way was I going to church.

Back in my teen years, I did a little runway modeling. I was always tall and thin and so I got into modeling when I was seventeen, but I wasn't serious about it. I only wanted to party and get high. I didn't care about much of anything else.

One day, while living in Charlotte, I walked into a dress boutique. The lady behind the desk was the owner and designer. She began to chat with me and asked immediately, "Do you do any modeling?" I told her, "Yes, but it's been a couple years." She continued to ask if I would model her dresses for her at an upcoming show in Atlanta. I was thrilled at the opportunity, since at the current time I didn't have a job. We began a friendship. This woman was a Christian, and every time I saw her or talked to her, she invited me to church. I continually told her, "No, thank you" but, she wouldn't stop. So, finally I agreed to go just to get her to stop inviting me.

That Sunday morning was beautiful, as my new boyfriend and I went to the later service. It was a huge church, with a couple thousand members. There was no way I was going to find my friend, I thought. But, honestly, I didn't even want her to know I was there. We were early and so we had to wait for first service to end before entering the sanctuary for second service. I made a beeline for the balcony and the furthest seat away from the pulpit. It was dark up there and God wouldn't be able to see me or find me. (Yes, these were my real thoughts.)

I can't tell you much about the worship service, or even what the pastor's message was, except that he preached my life. He preached my life. From my childhood abuse and raising myself, from being abandoned and alone to committing adultery and living with someone who was not my husband—it was all me. I was floored. I was crying the whole time. I couldn't believe it. How did this man know my life? And why was he looking at me the whole time? (Now, you know that ain't even true!) There is no way he could see me in the third-level balcony, but I would have sworn that he was looking at me while preaching my life. It was crazy. After service, I said to my boyfriend, "Didn't that affect you?" He replied, "It sure hit home." But he had no emotion. He was nonchalant about the whole thing, and I couldn't understand how he was not affected like I was.

I couldn't shake what I was feeling in my spirit. I needed to get out of my situation as soon as possible. I called my mom crying and told her about my experience. She told me to just come home to Texas. God was calling me and I needed to obey. So, I packed one small suitcase and left everything else. I left all my furniture, most of my clothes and shoes, my car, my dish-ware and glasses, pictures, photo albums......everything. And I left. The Tuesday after Sunday church, I got on a plane and flew back to San Antonio and never looked back. I didn't go to church on that Sunday; I think I was too scared. But I went the follow-ing Wednesday night and He met me at the altar. I didn't pray any certain prayer, and I can't remember the sermon, I just re-member pouring myself out to the Lord that Wednesday night and He met me right where I was. He didn't ask me to change before I came to Him, He just said come and be filled. Come and be changed. Come and be transformed. Come and be renewed. Come and be healed. Just come.

That was twenty years ago, and I have never looked back. I have never walked away and I have never back slid. But, I have fallen. The difference is now He is there to pick me up.

"For a righteous man falls seven times and rises again, but the wicked are overthrown by calamity" **Proverbs 24:16.**

"The steps of a [good] man are directed *and* established by the Lord when He delights in his way [and He busies Himself with his every step]. Though he falls, he shall not be utterly cast down, for the Lord grasps his hand in support *and* upholds him" **Psalm 37:23-24.**

When was the last time you fell? Or are you on the ground right now and you can't get up? Call out to Him! He is waiting to hear from you. He is longing to help you. He wants to pick you up. He wants to set your feet on solid ground. He wants to get you moving again in the right direction, His direction. His way. His path. Let him help you! He is *all* you need! Get up. Brush yourself off. Keep going. You will make it! There is a victory waiting for you at the finish line. Just because you fall, it doesn't make you a failure. You and God can do anything, overcome anything, climb any mountain, cross any sea. It's time to rise!

Chapter 22

Maximize the Consequences

I have made a lifetime commitment to running. Why? You ask. I will tell you "why." Because I care about my cardiovascular health. Running increases circulation. Over time, it will decrease cholesterol (along with a healthy eating plan), lower blood pressure, and increase the overall efficiency of the heart. What do I mean by this? The average healthy heart has 60–80 beats per minute, BPM. The athletic heart usually runs at 60 BPM at rest, and a *really* healthy heart can have as low as 40–50 BPM. My heart rate is right around 47 beats per minute at rest. My heart doesn't have to work as hard as an unfit person to circulate my blood. It can produce the same outcome (circulate blood and oxygen to every cell of my body) as a person in poorer health. This makes my heart more efficient—it does less work to produce the same outcome. Make sense?

I remind myself that I want to maintain my cardiovascular health as I age. I "maximize the consequences" of not running. As I age, I gain weight, lose muscle mass, have joint pain, etc., and I want to do whatever I can to stay off these things as long as possible. I remind my husband of these facts about aging every time he doesn't want to run. I remind him of the worst-case scenario of having bad cardiovascular health, therefore "maximizing the consequences."

I think most people don't want to confront their health issues, and they end up minimizing them. I know a lot of people who haven't put one thought into their health when they were young, and are now suffering their own personal "worst-case scenario" for it. And even now, they still don't want to do what it takes by disciplining themselves to eat right, exercise, stop smoking, drinking, etc. They'd rather take a pill to ease the symptoms. Sound familiar?

Now, apply this to your spiritual walk. How about the next time you want to do something that you know you shouldn't be doing—you *maximize* the consequences of what could happen if you went through with this act. For example, if you struggle with alcohol, take into consideration what will happen if you go to a party where everyone is drinking. Maximize the consequences of your drinking. Indulgent drinking leads to ruined lives, addiction, DUI's and possibly an alcohol related death, and lest we forget that drunkenness is a sin of the flesh according to Galatians 5:21, separating us from the Lord. Yet, I think most of us humans minimize the consequences. If you struggle with alcohol, it is highly possible that you will not be able to abstain, and yet we say to ourselves, "I can handle my alcohol. I won't get drunk. Maybe I won't even drink". Does the very worst possible scenario always happen? No. But it is always a possibility. Think about it.

"The year before I came to the Lord, I committed adultery." It took me a long time to be able to say that. I made excuses all the time. Yes, I was in a bad marriage. Yes, he was verbally abusive. Yes, he went to hit me one time and I fell on the floor in terror and learned to just shut up after that. But, I had committed adultery. I was the one who ran off with another person. I left behind hurt and pain. It wasn't until I came to the Lord that I realized the fullness of what I had done, and became aware of the pain I had caused to someone else. It's called Godly sorrow.

> "For godly grief *and* the pain God is permitted
> to direct, produce a repentance that leads *and*
> contributes to salvation *and* deliverance from evil,
> and it never brings regret; but worldly grief (the
> hopeless sorrow that is characteristic of the pagan
> world) is deadly [breeding and ending in death]"
> **2 Corinthians 7:10.**

The world's outlook on sorrow comes from the mindset of children. It's an "Oops, I got caught, sorry" perspective by and large. If you have children, you know what I mean. Try making one sibling apologize to another after getting "caught in the act." It comes out like a snotty, whiny, unapologetic "Sorrrreeee!" (Insert your own child's whiny voice here.) This is not godly repentance. This is an "I'm sorry until the next time" apology. The problem is that most people do not want to confront their own sin, and so they minimize how they hurt someone or how they've hurt the Lord, whining, "I'm sorreeee!" By doing this, they are minimizing their perception of consequences, which—depending on the hurt caused or the sin against Go—may be severe.

This world we live in has a blanket mentality of "Just live and do what makes you feel good." We minimize our sins, refusing to repent with godly sorrow before Him. Because we refuse to examine our hearts, bringing them open before the Lord so He can search us and "see if there is any wickedness in us," we end up walking down a path to destruction. Let me give you an example from Scripture: King David. As many of you may know, David had an affair with Bathsheba. To hide his sin, he had her husband killed and made Bathsheba his wife. It took a year for him to repent. Even then, it was only because the prophet, Nathan, was sent to show him his sin. For a whole year, David minimized his sin, tried to cover up his sin, not understanding there were consequences. And the consequences for David were severe. He lost his child, even after intense prayer and fasting. But that wasn't everything. Soon his sin affected all of Israel. (Read 2 Samuel Chapters 11 and 12 for the full story.) Believe it or not, your sins can affect others. It is not always about you. Besides all that, others are watching you and following your running path. Are you living a life that displays heavenly citizenship? If not, have you considered the effect it could have on others?

Whatever happened to living by the creed, "You are your brother's keeper?" Jesus had some good words to say on this:

> "Why do you see the speck that is in your brother's eye but do not notice *or* consider the beam [of timber] that is in your own eye? Or how can you say to your brother, 'Brother, allow me to take out the speck that is in your eye,' when you yourself do not see the beam that is in your own eye? You actor (pretender, hypocrite)! First take the beam out of your own eye, and then you will see clearly to take out the speck that is in your brother's eye"
> **Luke 6:41-42.**

Jesus is not telling us to never say anything to our brother about his sin. He said that the Pharisees and hypocrites walked around pointing everyone's sin out without getting themselves right first. They didn't have the right heart condition. Jesus tells us that we are to help our brother in Christ, but first make sure we have repented of our own wrong doing. Bingo! There it is—and the truth shall set you free! However, we typically don't want to take a hard look, examine our hearts, and repent. This is not an easy thing to do, but it is necessary in order to keep our hearts pure before the Lord. It is time to get real if you are going to run your race well.

> ˉLet the [latter] one be sure that whoever turns a sinner from his evil course will save [that one's] soul from death and will cover a multitude of sins [procure the pardon of the many sins committed by the convert]" James 5:20.

Do not forget that James here is writing to "the church," the body of believers. He is specifically talking about a wandering brother or sister in Christ.

Therefore, maximize the consequences of not confronting your own sin. Your sin has consequences. Every choice has an outcome, for good or for bad. Yes! You can be completely forgiven, but you may still have to live with certain consequences from your actions. David was not immune from his actions of adultery and murder, even though he was completely forgiven and fully loved by God. Examine your heart and your actions. Are you causing others to stumble? Are you turning others from the Lord? Are you allowing a brother/sister in Christ to wander down that wide path to destruction? What are the consequences of your actions, or in this case, non-action?

My husband and I started our marriage debt free. That's right, we had one vehicle that was paid off, we rented a townhome, and we had no credit card debt. Over the course of eleven years, we got ourselves into a huge financial pit. Neither of us had been taught how to budget or to be good stewards of money. If we wanted something, instead of delaying our gratification by saving up, we would just charge it to our credit card. You see, we did not maximize the consequences of our spending. We have spent the last seven years paying "stupid tax" (interest) in order to dig ourselves out of debt. We never thought about how our out-of-control spending was going to affect us in the future.

What is out of control in your life? Is it your eating? Are you borderline diabetic? Do you tipper on obesity? Before you take another bite of that triple chocolate fudge brownie, think about how it can affect your body in the future. Do you have a spending problem? Before you swipe that credit card or press "place order" on one of an endless stream of online retail sites, maximize the consequences. Think about having to declare bankruptcy and/or losing the ability to purchase a new home. Next time you see your brother fall into sexual sin, maximize the consequences to them. An affair, for example, cannot only create unbearable pain for its victims upon discovery, but it can result in an unplanned pregnancy, a sexual disease, the loss of a job, the loss of family and friends. People rack up so many lies during affairs that oftentimes their health is affected adversely by insomnia, high blood pressure, depression (to name a few). Perhaps the issue isn't infidelity but lack of control—sleeping around. This next time could spell out an HIV death sentence, or worse—an eternal death sentence. Be warned, though! When you begin to speak life into others and the truth of God's Word to a wandering brother, they may come against you and cast some stones. Not even the apostles were immune from a stoning.

Let me ask you a serious question: Have you ever been stoned? Paul was stoned. Stephen was stoned. They tried to stone Jesus. Peter was crucified upside down. James had his head chopped off—all persecuted for their outspoken faith. I have been stoned. I have had huge stones hurled at me for preaching and teaching the truth. I have been called a "hypocrite" and a "wolf in sheep's clothing" for telling someone they were on the path to destruction. I've been falsely accused of being unloving, unkind, intolerant, and full of hate. I've been hit over the head with accusations like "You spend the tithe on your shoes and jewelry" and "You are a false prophet." Need I go on? Once you begin to actually walk out the Word and live and speak the truth, some stones will be hurled your way. Now more than ever you need to be preaching the truth of God's Word! We are closer to Jesus's return now more than ever before. It's time to reach out to your wandering brothers and sisters in Christ and bring them back! Do not let them be lost forever. Even if they stone you, keep speaking the truth because someone's eternity depends on it.

Chapter 23

Rest When It Gets Too Hot

My poor doggy is getting old. He's got a silver streak of fur down his back, he grunts when he lies down, and he grunts when he gets up. I've started to give him glucosamine for his aches and pains, but he still cannot run two days in a row. When he first started out running, for the first seven years of his life, he was dragging me five miles and ready for more. He'll be ten this year and he still loves to run, but I have to be more careful. He always loved running in the rain, snow, in the hot of summer, the dead of winter; you name the weather and he could run. But now he's just too old to run in the heat. Anything above seventy degrees is too much for him: "The spirit is willing, but the flesh is weak." I'm losing my running partner.

I, too, have noticed the older I get, I can't run in the heat either. In my twenties, I would run in ninety-nine-degree weather at four or five in the afternoon with no problems. Now, I think I would collapse with heat stroke. I used to roof houses with my stepdad in Texas, and it would be 100 degrees and I wouldn't even need a break. All day! Papa would take a break for lunch and lie down in the shade for a little nap, and I would work right through. Of course, he has a good twenty years on me (of both age and wisdom). I was young, dumb, and thought I knew everything. What twenty-something-year-old doesn't think they know everything?

I recount another times in my life where I refused to rest or take a break, or be weary of circumstances; I wasn't always so lucky. After the birth of my son, Gabriel, I was supposed to rest until I stopped bleeding. But, I didn't. I tried to go for a run. Consequently, I was out of commission for a week or so longer. Another time was after my gall bladder surgery—I was tired after lying around for two days, so I tried to vacuum. My friend Molly, who was helping me for a couple days, set me straight. "What are you doing, Crystal? You have inner stitches, and if you undo those I will *never* come back to help you out again." Yes, ma'am. I got back in bed immediately.

I am a hard worker, always have been, but as I get older and somewhat wiser, sometimes I have to rest when it gets too hot, or circumstances dictate. Trust me, I am still struggling with this "rest" thing.

Last summer, my family went to Idaho to visit my husband's grandfather. There's a beautiful four-mile route that I love to run whenever we go there. So, before an all-day adventure at the local water park, Matt and I went on that run. Even just after sunrise, you could tell it was going to be a scorcher that day.

Well, we spent all day running around the water park, having fun. I wasn't staying hydrated. I guess I just wasn't thinking about drinking water while I was having fun and playing in the water. We left at the end of the day and stopped to get frozen yogurt.

While we were eating, I felt my heart go into a funny rhythm. Now, I've had several panic attacks in my twenties and thirties and so I knew what a panic attack felt like—this was different. We got back to the house and I tried to do deep breathing to slow my heart down, but nothing would correct it. Matt took me to the nearby fire station. The medic did an EKG and told me to go to the hospital. I got in right away. They gave me an IV with cardiac meds to slow down my heart rate and help it get back into rhythm. But my heart would not get back into its natural beat. The last resort was to "shock" my heart. (I told you this story previously, but stick with me for a moment.)

For the first time ever I think, I had no fear. I was perfectly at peace. My life was in my Father's hands. My heart beat was in His hands. Matt left the room, they sedated me, and then they shocked me four times for my heart rhythm to return. Matt said I came out of anesthesia prophesying the Lord's Word to all the doctors and the nurses in the room, but I don't remember. I was diagnosed with AFib and was put on a beta blocker and was told I couldn't run for two weeks! Ugh! The agony of it all! I had to actually rest for two whole weeks until I could get in to see a cardiologist in my area.

Rest? For me the struggle is real! But God requires us to rest because He knows our bodies need rest in order to run our race. Resting in the Lord produces patience and trust in God's ability to take care of you and handle the circumstances you are going through. Not only does your physical body need rest, your mind and spirit need rest as well. In resting, your spirit is restored and revived. Resting clears your head of troubles and allows you to hear the voice of the Lord clearly. I love this portion of Psalm 23, "He *makes* me to lie down in green pastures." I hear this psalm and think of the times my kids would act up because they were tired and needed a nap and so I would make them lie down and rest.

"Six days shall work be done, but the seventh day is the Sabbath of rest, a holy convocation *or* assembly by summons. You shall do no work on that day; it is the Sabbath of the Lord in all your dwellings" **Leviticus 23:3.**

If you're anything like me, you find it hard to rest, but God has ordained for you to rest and refresh your body and spirit. Are you weary? Rest in the Lord. Sometimes, you need to take a break and just rest in His arms. Listen to your body and listen to the Holy Spirit.

"Be still *and* rest in the Lord; wait for Him *and* patiently lean yourself upon Him; fret not yourself because of him who prospers in his way, because of the man who brings wicked devices to pass" **Psalm 37:7.**

I remember when I first came to the Lord. I was a sad, shell of a person. I was completely empty. Empty of love. Empty of hope. Empty, empty, empty. I needed to be filled. I kid you not, I spent three hours a day in prayer and reading my Bible. I would memorize Scripture for hours at a time. I stopped going out with anyone, anywhere. I went to work, college, and church. I needed to be filled. I spent three years with this same routine. I needed to rest in His presence. I needed to be loved. I needed hope. I needed forgiveness. I needed restoration. I needed deliverance. I needed Him. Period.

He is your Healer. He is your Restorer. He is your Deliverer. But, you have to get in His presence and rest. Maybe you've been running a long time and you are tired and weary. Rest in his presence! It worked for Elijah.

"But he himself went a day's journey into the wilderness and came and sat down under a lone broom *or* juniper tree and asked that he might die. He said, 'It is enough; now, O Lord, take away my life; for I am no better than my fathers.' As he lay asleep under the broom *or* juniper tree, behold, an angel touched him and said to him, 'Arise and eat.' He looked, and behold, there was a cake baked on the coals, and a bottle of water at his head. And he ate and drank and lay down again. The angel of the Lord came the second time and touched him and said, 'Arise and eat, for the journey is too great for you.' So he arose and ate and drank, and went in the strength of that food forty days and nights to Horeb, the mount of God" 1 **Kings 19:4-8.**

Elijah was plumb worn out and weary. He lay down, physically and spiritually exhausted, ready to die. But He rested in the Lord. God fed him, strengthened him, and sent him running again for forty days and nights. And he did this while thriving off a few small meals. That's some strength! That's some power! All from resting in his presence.

There are certain times and seasons when the command to "Be still" will be mandatory. You will miss the voice of the Lord if you refuse to be still, rest and listen.

I remember when Matt and I wanted to start the church. I say "We" wanted to start the church because "we" thought it was the right time. Our plan was to buy a house and start the church in our home. We tried for months, running here and there looking at homes, land, manufactured homes—anything that looked good and was big enough to plant a church in. Every door, and I mean *every* door, was slammed in our faces. With one house we were going to pay full price plus closing costs *and* we still didn't get it. We were extremely tired and frustrated. After that, we had to reevaluate our situation.

See, we were running very fast, but not staying still long enough to really hear His voice. After some wise counsel, we stopped running and just started resting and praying. Peace flooded us and we rested in His presence, waiting on Him to give us the go ahead to continue running the race.

Be still in his presence and let Him speak to you. Be still and let Him refresh your soul. When life gets too hot, be still. When you've done all you can and all he's told you, just be still and rest. You have a race to run, but sometimes you have to stop and tie your shoes so you do not trip and fall.

Chapter 24

The Grass *is* Greener on the Other Side

People tell us "The grass is greener on the other side" when we're considering doing something we shouldn't, something that looks appealing from our vantage. Well, the grass is not greener on the other side!

Matt and I run through a three-and-half-mile route through a neighborhood. We do a quarter-mile warm up and cool down, so we've planned the route with a starting and stopping place that gives us three full miles of running. We were running this route the other day. It was a beautiful June morning, sixty-five and sunny, the perfect weather to run in. Along this route, we came around a corner that leads to a plush, green, exceptionally-manicured lawn. An elderly couple live there. They are constantly clipping, mowing, seeding, weeding, trimming, and blowing this lawn. One time, I saw the woman out there actually clipping her grass with a pair of sheers! Amazing. Matt and I have always both been enamored by this lawn. It's absolutely beautiful. We continued on our run.

We turned around at the corner and started our way back. (We don't always do a "there and back," but that day we did.) That's when we noticed the lawn directly across the street from the gorgeous plush lawn. It was yellow, uneven, full of weeds, had patches of dirt everywhere, and it wasn't mowed or trimmed. "I'll bet they (the elderly couple) love that guy," my husband said. We laughed and kept running. But that got me thinking about my own lawn. It didn't look that bad, but it certainly did not look like the elderly couple's lawn. But then, we only put product on our lawn maybe once a month. We water it, but not regularly. Our lawn looks green from a distance. Up close, it's full of moss and clovers, loads of them. It's patchy in places and yellow in places. We keep it trimmed and mowed. I would love to have a beautiful lawn, but I'm not willing to do what it takes.

It's no different for the runner. I have a runner's body. Yes, I'm thin and in shape. "Must be nice," you say? Well, I eat right and put in the miles every week to maintain my runner's body. The grass might seem greener "on my side," but it's really not. I've put in the work my whole adult life.

Are you connecting the dots? This is so much like your spiritual walk. Do you look at other people's lives and get mad? Has "must be nice" become your slogan? Here's a question: are you willing to do what it takes?

The people that I have seen be blessed by God are those who obey His Word, in all areas. Are you experiencing weeds in your finances? Well then, you need to tithe. You don't like that word do you. Tithe. This means give a tenth of your income to God. This goes to your church, not a good will organization. It goes to the place where you get fed, your storehouse. The place where the seed of the gospel is being planted. An offering is anything on top of that: missions, good will organizations, help ministries, etc.

> "Will a man rob *or* defraud God? Yet you rob *and* defraud Me. But you say, 'In what way do we rob *or* defraud You?' [You have withheld your] tithes and offerings" **Malachi 3:8.**

I've been tithing for twenty-plus years, ever since I've been saved. I'm not telling you this as a pastor, I am telling you this as a sister in Christ. Do you want a plush lawn? How about a runner's body? Then you need to tithe. Otherwise, the devourer will keep stealing your money.

> "'You are cursed with the curse, for you are robbing Me, even this whole nation. Bring all the tithes (the whole tenth of your income) into the storehouse, that there may be food in My house, and prove Me now by it,' says the Lord of hosts, 'If I will not open the windows of heaven for you and pour you out a blessing, that there shall not be room enough to receive it. And I will rebuke the devourer [insects and plagues] for your sakes and he shall not destroy the fruits of your ground, neither shall your vine drop its fruit before the time in the field,' says the Lord of hosts" **Malachi 3:9-11.**

For all you tithing-is-under-the-law types, perhaps you need to go all the way back to the beginning with Cain and Abel. Abel brought his first fruits; he brought his "best of the best," while Cain brought God his leftovers. Cain did not bring God his first fruit; therefore, God did not have respect for him. God loved Cain, but He did not accept his offering. We see the same heart in Abraham as in Abel. Abraham brought his first fruits to the priest Melchizedek. He brought his "tithe," the top ten percent of what he had to give. Again, first fruits and pre-law. Likewise, Jesus told His followers that there were blessings for obeying God's Word.

> "But He said, 'Blessed (happy and to be envied) rather are those who hear the Word of God and obey *and* practice it!'" **Luke 11:28.**

Listen and obey the words of Jesus. There are blessings for obedience. He utters the same words of the OT: "The blessing if you obey the commandments of the Lord your God which I command you this day; And the curse if you will not obey the commandments of the Lord your God, but turn aside from the way which I command you this day to go after other gods, which you have not known" Deuteronomy 11:27-28.

God is a blesser of those who seek after Him, to know Him and to obey Him. Where else aren't you obeying God? Are you living with someone who's not your spouse? Are you in a relationship you shouldn't be? Are you going places the Lord has told you not to go? Are you drinking too much alcohol? (Drunkenness is a sin) Are you harboring a grudge? When you are disobedient, you are out of the safety and security of the Father. What area are you leaving open to the devil?

I struggled with drinking; I liked it too much. I liked the way it tasted and I liked the way it made me feel. But after I came to the Lord, He removed that from me and I didn't touch a drop of alcohol for many years. Slowly, though, I let it creep back in.

I used it as an anxiety reducer. I wasn't getting drunk anymore; but rather, I'd have a few drinks to "calm the spirit." I lied to myself that I wasn't sinning because I wasn't getting drunk. However, God told me, "Do not drink at all, Crystal." I wasn't even allowed a taste. It went on and on like that for about two years. I would be okay for a month and then instead of going to the Lord to help with my anxiety, I would go to alcohol and that old spirit would come back on me. It was a vicious cycle and I kept disobeying God and opening the door for Satan to come in and run all over me.

The Lord posed a question to me, "Crystal, do you love alcohol more than Me?" That's when I broke. I cried out to God and made a vow that I would never touch another drink. He was more important to me than a glass of wine, and if I never drank again, He was enough.

It just so happened that right after that vow, I was in Texas for my twenty-year class reunion. I had been thinking of getting some kind of token to remind me of my vow. I happened to be looking through a James Avery jewelry magazine that my mom had, and I found a sterling silver ring, a band that had *I am my beloved's and my beloved is mine* inscribed in Hebrew. I told my mom all about this struggle and the ring I wanted as a token and a vow of my commitment. The next day she took me to the James Avery store and they had one, my size, in stock. The real kicker to this whole story was that my mom purchased it for me. I love my mom, but (and she knows this), she is pretty tightfisted. She doesn't purchase expensive items. It meant the world to me. The devil got a black eye that day! And that beautiful ring on my finger served as an easy reminder not to drink at my reunion. It gave me strength. Plus, there was an added blessing from the Lord with my mother and our relationship for my obedience. Are you willing to obey the Lord in all areas? We are often like the rich young ruler in Scripture. He obeyed the Lord in "all these commandments" yet, there was one thing he lacked. Jesus is always into probing the one area of disobedience, that one area which we have not submitted to Him. If you want the blessings of the Lord, then obedience is required for every area. Stop looking longingly at another's lawn. When you are unwilling to be obedient in even the smallest detail, how can you expect your lawn to mirror theirs?

Jesus said this to rebuke the devil in the wilderness:

> "And Jesus replied to him, It is written, Man shall not live *and* be sustained by (on) bread alone *but by every word and expression of God*" **Luke 4:4.**

He intends for us to live by the Word of God, every Word of God. The whole Bible. The whole counsel of God from Genesis to Revelation.

Do you want the favor of God on your life? Obey Him from the heart. You're going to have to pull some weeds. You're going to have to start running if you want a runner's physique. You need to start some training and discipline today.

> "But refuse *and* avoid irreverent legends (profane and impure and godless fictions, mere grandmothers' tales) and silly myths, *and* express your disapproval of them. Train yourself toward godliness (piety), [keeping yourself spiritually fit]" **1 Timothy 4:7.**

You have to stop thinking about what you don't have; You have to stop looking at what others do have. This mentality breeds covetousness and jealousy, and these two things are poison to your soul. Sow seeds of righteousness and you will reap a harvest in time.

> "And let us not lose heart *and* grow weary *and* faint in acting nobly *and* doing right, for in due time *and* at the appointed season we shall reap, if we do not loosen *and* relax our courage *and* faint" **Galatians 6:9.**

The grass is greener when you obey from the heart—the grass looks greener on both sides when you live like this. You have a race to run, but it's not a race for your own desires; it's God's race that He designed for you. Run in complete obedience and the favor of the Lord will chase you down.

Chapter 25

A Runner is Disciplined

It takes dedication, perseverance, and discipline to become a runner. Wikipedia defines discipline as—*the suppression of base desires, and is usually understood to be synonymous with restraint and self-control. Self-discipline is to some extent a substitute for motivation.* Restraint. Self-control. Paul tells us that self-control is a fruit of having the Spirit living within you, meaning that the born-again Christian is able to control themselves and their actions through the power of the Spirit. In order to run your race, you have to exercise self-control.

I had a friend that ran track for the University of Texas at San Antonio (UTSA). She was very fast and very thin, but the coach wanted her to shed two more pounds. He said that by dropping those two pounds, she could shave a couple of seconds of her mile time. I was like, "Where are you going to lose two pounds?!" She was diligent and disciplined and after about a month, she was able to lose those two pounds, which ultimately shaved almost five seconds off her time! Amazing. But, it was not easy. She couldn't cut too many calories, she needed the energy. She didn't want to lose muscle because you never want to lose your muscle mass and compromise muscle tone—people who exercise work hard for that benefit. She stuck to a super strict diet and upped her running routine.

Just at my level, it takes discipline and self-control to eat healthy, energy-giving food and in order to run my twenty miles a week. It takes me getting up and preparing myself to run. I have to run before my breakfast, so sometimes, I am tired, and I run if I'm tired. I run if I'm sore. I run if it's raining. I run if it's hot. I run if it's cold. I run indoors. I run outdoors—and let me tell you: the weather in Seattle is crazy. Matt says the weather in the Pacific Northwest is like a psychotic girlfriend. She's dark and dreary for days on end, and raining and ugly, and then just when you decide you've had enough and you want to leave her, she turns sunny and blue. "Oh, look at me! I am beautiful!" and you take her back. Yes, I even run when she is mean and nasty. I run because a runner is disciplined.

> Likewise, the Saint of God is also disciplined. Paul says: "But [like a boxer] I buffet my body [handle it roughly, discipline it by hardships] and subdue it, for fear that after proclaiming to others the Gospel *and* things pertaining to it, I myself should become unfit [not stand the test, be unapproved and rejected as a counterfeit]" 1 Corinthians 9:27.

Paul understood that even though he preached the gospel *all over* the continent to many people and nations, he could be rejected and counted, as King James says, a "castaway," for allowing his flesh to dictate and control his life. I would be remiss if I didn't share certain Scriptures with you concerning the life lived in the flesh. Remember, Paul is not speaking to those who do not know Christ. He is speaking to those in the Galatian Church; those who claim to know Jesus—people like you and me.

> "Now the works of the flesh are evident, which
> are: adultery, fornication, uncleanness, lewdness,
> idolatry, sorcery, hatred, contentions, jealousies,
> outbursts of wrath, selfish ambitions, dissensions,
> heresies, envy, murders, drunkenness, revelries, and
> the like; of which I tell you beforehand, just as I also
> told *you* in time past, that those who practice such
> things will not inherit the kingdom of God"
> **Galatians 5:19-21.**

> "Do you not know that the unrighteous will not
> inherit the kingdom of God? Do not be deceived.
> Neither fornicators, nor idolaters, nor adulterers,
> nor homosexuals, nor sodomites, nor thieves,
> nor covetous, nor drunkards, nor revilers, nor
> extortioners will inherit the kingdom of God"
> **1 Corinthians 6:9-10.**

> And if that is not enough for you to believe it, hear
> the words of Jesus: "Then He who sat on the throne
> said, 'Behold, I make all things new.' And He said
> to me, 'Write, for these words are true and faithful.'
> And He said to me, 'It is done! I am the Alpha and
> the Omega, the Beginning and the End. I will give
> of the fountain of the water of life freely to him who
> thirsts. He who overcomes shall inherit all things,
> and I will be his God and he shall be My son. But
> the cowardly, unbelieving, abominable, murderers,
> sexually immoral, sorcerers, idolaters, and all liars
> shall have their part in the lake which burns with
> fire and brimstone, which is the second death'"
> **Revelation 21:5-8.**

Life in the Spirit overcomes all these sins, but you have to discipline the flesh. He gives us His Spirit as our Helper. The Helper to overcome the devil. The Helper to overcome sin. You have to say "No" to the flesh and "Yes" to the Spirit. Is this a struggle? Yes! Yes! Yes! It is a bloody battle. I struggle and fight against my flesh every single day. However, I will tell you this: the more you walk in the Spirit and obey His leading, the easier it gets. The things I struggled with twenty years or even ten years ago, I have overcome because I would not allow that sin to have control over me.

Let me give you an example. When my children were younger, I had them both in swimming lessons. I would take them every day and sit and read, while the instructor taught them. I started to notice how the young man that was teaching them to swim would stare at me and go out of his way to talk to me. I entertained it for a little while because I didn't realize that he was flirting. Eventually, it started to make me uncomfortable and I removed the kids from swimming until another instructor was on staff. I never did anything wrong, but I have learned to never say never, because I believe that given the right place and the right time, we are prone to do just about anything if we are not continually disciplining the flesh. The Bible says, "Flee fornication." This means to run fast away from anything that can be construed as sexual immorality. For the New Testament Christian, even the thought of adultery is sin. You cannot entertain any thought that is founded in the sinful flesh. A thought that is not taken captive leads to an action. I know people who've cheated on their spouse over a lot less than ongoing flirting. All it takes is one bad interaction with your spouse coupled with some good attention from another person. Run fast away from anything that can cause you to sin!

I can hear your thoughts: *What?! I have to be perfect and never, ever sin! How on earth do I do that?* This is not the case. There is a huge difference between "struggling against sin" and "giving yourself over to sin." I struggle. Hopefully, you struggle. And, as they say, "The struggle is real." As long as you and I are in this fleshly body, you are going to struggle against sin. The flesh wants to sin. But, when you were born again of the Spirit of God, you received a new nature—the nature of the Father. These two natures are contrary to each other. They are enemies.

> "For those who live according to the flesh set their minds on the things of the flesh, but those *who live* according to the Spirit, the things of the Spirit. For to be carnally minded *is* death, but to be spiritually minded *is* life and peace. Because the carnal mind *is* enmity against God; for it is not subject to the law of God, nor indeed can be" **Romans 8:5-7.**

Therefore, you will either surrender to Him and follow the leading of the Holy Spirit, or harden your heart, grieve the Spirit, put out His fire, and continue a life in the sinful fleshly nature. What's it going to be?

The Spirit wants to and longs to help you overcome. You were made to be an overcomer through the Spirit! Don't let one more day go by. today, if you will hear His voice, put to death that sinful nature once and for all! Paul tells us we are to reckon ourselves dead to sin and alive in Christ. Dead to sin! Alive in Christ! You have been given the gift of self-control. He helps you to overcome this nasty, stinking flesh in order that you would experience the victory of the cross.

"What shall we say then? Shall we continue in sin that grace may abound? Certainly not! How shall we who died to sin live any longer in it? Or do you not know that as many of us as were baptized into Christ Jesus were baptized into His death? Therefore we were buried with Him through baptism into death, that just as Christ was raised from the dead by the glory of the Father, even so we also should walk in newness of life. For if we have been united together in the likeness of His death, certainly we also shall be *in the likeness* of *His* resurrection, knowing this, that our old man was crucified with *Him,* that the body of sin might be done away with, that we should no longer be slaves of sin. For he who has died has been freed from sin. Now if we died with Christ, we believe that we shall also live with Him, knowing that Christ, having been raised from the dead, dies no more. Death no longer has dominion over Him. For *the death* that He died, He died to sin once for all; but *the life* that He lives, He lives to God. Likewise you also, reckon yourselves to be dead indeed to sin, but alive to God in Christ Jesus our Lord" **Romans 6:1-11.**

Did you just read that? If you died with Him, you have been set free from sin and made alive in Christ. There is nothing good that comes from living a life in the flesh. I repeat, nothing good, only destruction. But, a disciplined life dictated by self-control, lived according to the Spirit brings everlasting life, joy, peace, and freedom.

Chapter 26

The Runner's High

I am addicted to running! Seriously, it is almost shameful. I start to feel "bound up" if I go more than a day or two without running. And car trips—forget about it!

We like to have family vacations during the summer, where we travel from place to place visiting family, friends, Disneyland, and national monuments. After one day of riding in the car, I am jonesing for a run. I need my runner's fix! I am addicted to the way running makes me feel. If we stay at a hotel, it needs to be one with an exercise room, so I can get up early and hit the treadmill, so all the stress and pent up energy can be released and I can breathe. Hi, my name is Crystal and I am addicted to a runner's euphoric high.

This is from an article on Web MD titled, "Runner's High: Is it Real?" dated 3 March 2016.

> "Through the blood, sweat, and tears, many runners report that their favorite trickand part of the reason they wake morning after morning to pound the pavementis what is referred to as runner's high. 'Psychologically, runners may experience euphoria, a feeling of being invincible, a reduced state of discomfort or pain, and even a loss in sense of time while running,' says Jesse Pittsley, PhD, president of the American Society for Exercise Physiologists."

This is a real thing! There is definitely an addiction to running. You get addicted to how running makes you *feel*. I can attest to this phenomenon. On my running days, I feel more energetic and peppy. I'm in a state of euphoria. On days I do not run, I feel down and depressed, which is why I am constantly hitting the pavement. I think my hubby may be starting to experience a little of the runner's high. He's been actually wanting to run! He tells me he notices that he has more energy on the days he runs. Yes! Finally!

I have noticed this same phenomenon in the Church.

There are people that just follow around a minister or a move of the Holy Spirit. They are constantly looking for that next "high," that next touch of the Spirit, but never getting fully grounded on God's Word. There is a difference between seeking the Lord for who He is and seeking Him for what He can do for you. This second type of person is always seeking that "high" of the Lord, seeking His spiritual gifts and *feelings*, but never really seeking to be in a relationship with Jesus. I was saved in a Pentecostal church. I am so grateful for my salvation experience and introduction to God. I was taught about the gifts of the Spirit: speaking in tongues, prophecy, words of knowledge and wisdom, healings, etc. I sought the gifts of the Spirit because I so longed to be able to pray in tongues (pray in the Spirit). We had some pretty wild services! I didn't mind until I began to dig into God's Word and found out about the Corinthian Church, and how Paul told them they were disorderly and fleshly. What I began to notice was that speaking in tongues alone does not make you spiritual.

It's interesting that most of Paul's letters were written about problems going on in the churches, especially the Corinthian Church.

> "And I, brethren, could not speak to you as to
> spiritual people but as to carnal, as to babes in
> Christ. I fed you with milk and not with solid food; for
> until now you were not able to receive it, and even
> now you are still not able; for you are still carnal.
> For where there are envy, strife, and divisions among
> you, are you not carnal and behaving like mere men?
> For when one says, 'I am of Paul,' and another, 'I am
> of Apollos,' are you not carnal?" **1 Corinthians 3:1-4.**

These Corinthian Christians spoke in tongues and prophesied, but Paul said that they were still carnal Christians. Sure, they spoke in tongues and "felt" the Spirit, but they still had selfish divisions, the world's philosophy, jealousy and quarreling, pride, immorality, trivial lawsuits, attendance at idolatrous festivals and practiced rejecting apostolic teaching. They abused the gifts of the Spirit and distorted the gospel.

Like in Paul's day, this is still going on. People get touched by God, speak in tongues, prophecy, get healed, or "fall out" under the Spirit, but never get grounded on God's word and so they move from "feeling" to "feeling." In short, they become yo-yo Christians. They become addicted to feeling a move of God. They are easily upset. They are easily shaken. They are easily offended, because they have learned to be led by their feelings and are therefore still carnal.

> "Great peace have they who love Your law; nothing
> shall offend them or make them stumble" **Psalm 119:165.**

I know what you would ask: Is being addicted to God's Spirit wrong? No way. I love God's presence. I am addicted to His presence. I love feeling the Holy Spirit. I love praying in tongues and prophesying. I love the Holy Spirit. I cannot live without His presence in my life. But, you cannot allow that feeling (the runner's high) to lead you. People get a touch of the "tinglies" from the Lord and when they don't feel that the next time they are in church, they leave and try to find it somewhere else, like in another church, or they become sullen and depressed, maybe even start asking, "Why did God leave me?"

> I fell into this trap as a baby Christian, thinking that God left me because I didn't feel His presence "this Sunday" like I felt Him "last Sunday." This is being immature in the faith. The yo-yo Christian is happy when they feel God, but sad when they don't, and will spend the bulk of their energy chasing after the feeling, not unlike the runner's high. Always pursuing that next high. This leads to being lead by your emotions, thoughts, and opinions. The Book of Judges ends with this statement: "In those days there was no king in Israel; everyone did what was right in his own eyes" **Judges 21:25.**

If Jesus is not your King, then you will always do what seems right in your own eyes. Human feelings and opinions are a poor judge of what is good and right. As previously stated, the only good and right way is the Word of God. Of course, feelings are a part of our DNA. We were created to experience happiness, sadness, anger, etc. Yet our feelings are so often associated with our circumstances. My tire is flat and I am running late for work; hence, I am angry. In my anger, I lash out at my family and am justified because of my circumstances. Is this right according to God's Word? (This is a rhetorical question.) No, it is not right. I am allowed, of course, to feel anger, but I am not allowed to be controlled by my anger and lash out. We are to be led by the Spirit, not our own feelings.

"There is a way that seems right to a man,

But its end is the way of death" **Proverbs 14:12.**

You cannot be on the hunt for your next high feeling. The Book of Acts, Chapter 8 records Peter administering the baptism of the Holy Spirit by the laying on of hands and there is a man following his ministry called Simon the Sorcerer. Simon saw that the Holy Spirit was given through the laying on of the apostle's hands, and he offered to pay Peter for the power of the Spirit. Peter rebuked him. "You have neither part nor portion in this matter, for your heart is not right in the sight of God" **Acts 8:21.**

I think this happens a lot when people come in contact with the power of the Holy Spirit. They want what the Spirit can *give* or *do* for them, but not the Spirit Himself. So, they continue to seek after the gifts of God, instead of the Gift Giver. They go after that next manifestation, the next tingle. And all the time, their heart is still not right.

God wants you to be grounded. You need to be in a church that manifests the power of the Spirit and the people operate in the gifts of the Spirit, however you will not feel those "tinglies" every time you are in church. God wants you to be led by the Spirit (not by feeling the Spirit, but by obeying the Spirit) and grounded on His Word. Then, you will not be moved and you can grow and become spiritually mature in your faith.

"Therefore, laying aside all malice, all deceit, hypocrisy, envy, and all evil speaking, as newborn babes, desire the pure milk of the word, that you may grow thereby, if indeed you have tasted that the Lord is gracious" 1 Peter 2:1-3.

Don't fall into the trap of the yo-yo Christian. I equate it to a crash dieter. These people gain weight, go on a crash diet, lose weight, and then begin to eat unhealthy again. They've made no real-life change. The yo-yo Christian does the same thing in the spiritual sense. They will make changes in their walk, begin to read their Bible more and attend church regularly until they begin to feel better, and then go straight back to their old ways with no long-term, real-life changes. Christianity is a lifestyle, not a quick fix, not a crash diet.

Chapter 27

Sometimes You Have to Tell the Dog No

Ranger is getting old. It's really a sad thing to watch my lively, spunky puppy become an old man. The last time I took him on a long run was about six months ago. He pushed through it, but I could tell he was hurting. He loves his runs, always has. I got him home that day and he collapsed and didn't move for two days. Poor guy! I didn't realize how much pain he was really in. His glucosamine and aspirin keep him more comfortable. But it breaks my heart seeing him in this condition. When I go for my runs now, he still gets excited and follows me around until I leave, but then he sits in the upstairs window watching me as I round the corner. It's a sad sight to see and hard for me to leave him behind. He doesn't know what's good for him and, if I took him, he'd run until his hips gave out. Thankfully, I know what's good for him. He's a dog. He's a proverb and a parable.

> "As a dog returns to his vomit, so a fool returns to his folly" **Proverbs 26:11.**

And yes, I know it's gross, but he will eat his own vomit. I repeat, he doesn't know what's good for him and what will harm him.

Guess what? God says, "No." He knows what's good for me. Actually, He tells me "No" quite a bit. I have learned that He is really good at saying no, even if we earthly parents are not. He's a good, good Father. He knows what is good for us and what is not good for us. He knows what is harmful and what is safe. So, if He says "No," you can be sure that it is for a reason.

He gives you boundaries and limitations for our benefit, not His. I can think back on my life and still hear the many times He's told me "No" Sometimes I obeyed, other times I did not. I can tell you this: when God says no He means no. He will slam doors in your face. He will send a friend, pastor, or even a stranger to try to warn you. And if you persist, He will let you have your way. But, you will then have to face the consequences of forcing your own way into the picture over His.

When I was in junior high, I used to smoke a lot of pot. (Remember all those schools I went to in seventh and eighth grade?) I first tried marijuana when I was nine. At that time, my mother told me she didn't want me to smoke it behind her back, but that I could smoke it with her. I think in some, insane way, my mom wanted to know what I was doing and, if I was going to do it anyway, might as well be in front of her. This is faulty thinking.

Unlike how I was raised, we have rules in our house. For example, my children are not allowed to date. Now, some people would say that my kids going to date secretly, so I may as well let them. I believe this, too, is faulty thinking. I tell my children that they can sneak behind my back, but that God still knows and they will know that they are being rebellious and disobedient. My children also have an understanding that one day they will give an account of their life before the Lord. So, if they choose to be sneaky, they aren't really getting away with anything. These are our rules—mine and Matt's. Parents, you do not have to follow our rules; you make the rules for your own house. But, I will tell you to not allow the world to dictate what you can or cannot do with your children. Pray for guidance and make godly rules.

The tragedy of the nation of Israel was that they never listened when God told them no.

Therefore, as the Holy Spirit says:

> "Today, if you will hear His voice,
> Do not harden your hearts as in the rebellion,
> In the day of trial in the wilderness,
> Where your fathers tested Me, tried Me,
> And saw My works forty years.
> Therefore I was angry with that generation,
> And said, 'They always go astray in their heart,
> And they have not known My ways'"
> **Hebrews 3:7-10.**

He wrote out everything He wanted for them to do or do not. He only asked that his people would be faithful to follow and obey Him. sometimes, I think that would be a lot easier: "God, just write me out a list of things you do want me to do and things you don't want me to do." Yeah, well, that's not how it works. There are definite do's and do not's in the Bible, but with a lot of things, He just asks us to pray and seek His guidance and will. The Spirit is given to you in order to lead and guide in the path that God has for your life.

> "But the Comforter (Counselor, Helper, Intercessor, Advocate, Strengthener, Standby), the Holy Spirit, Whom the Father will send in My name [in My place, to represent Me and act on My behalf], He will teach you all things. And He will cause you to recall (will remind you of, bring to your remembrance) everything I have told you" **John 14:26.**

I will tell you that the Spirit will not give you any "new revelation" concerning the Word of God. I know people that seek God for an answer He has already given in His Word, and because they do not like that answer, they think He will change it. Sorry to inform you that God's Word is true, even in the 2000s. He still says what He means, and He means what He says.

> "So there are three witnesses in heaven: the Father, the Word and the Holy Spirit, and these three are One; and there are three witnesses on the earth: the Spirit, the water, and the blood; and these three agree [are in unison; their testimony coincides]"
> 1 John 5:7-8.

The Word and the Spirit are always in unison and agreement. If you think God has given you "yes" to something that's clearly a "no" in His Word, then you need to readjust your hearing aid.

Let me give you an example. I'm going to discuss a touchy subject for a minute: divorce. Why is the divorce rate so high in the church? Here's just a few reasons: the hardness of people's hearts, every man wants to do what is right in his own eyes, people don't want to have to control their flesh. Divorce is still not God's will for His people. Now, are there Biblical reasons for divorce? Absolutely. But I also believe that God's perfect will is divine forgiveness and softened hearts toward your spouse, no matter what they have done, even adultery. It can be done through the power of God. Hearts can be healed and mended. You are free to divorce in the case of adultery, this is in accordance with God's Word. But if you earnestly seek God on the matter, you might just get a "no." He might just want you to work through it. He might just ask you to forgive and take your spouse back. On the other hand, if you are seeking a divorce for no other reason than you are unhappy, you may not even get an answer, because it's already been written in His Word. Does God forgive divorce? Yes, if you repent. But, remember what I said about reaping the consequences of your actions? If you persist in having your own way, you may just find yourself in a worse situation.

I had been saved for about two years when I ran into an old friend from high school. We began hanging out and eventually dating, even though he was not a Christian. I knew I was not to be unequally yoked and so many of my good Christian friends tried to warn me about getting involved with him. He was a nice, decent, moral man, but he didn't love the Lord and had told me so on different occasions that the "church thing" and the "God thing" was good for me, but not for him. But, I continued to press my way because I was lonely. I rationalized that he was from God because I had known him since I was fifteen. Boy, what a lie I told myself!

After about two months of dating, we were at a family gathering for my mom's birthday and he popped the question. I had wondered why all his family was there.... I was dumbfounded, and after what seemed like a lifetime of a pause, I said, "Yes," even though I knew that was not the right answer. Immediately, I was convicted by the Holy Spirit. The rest of the week the Spirit was working on me, "No, no, no!" until I finally gave back the ring and we split up and went our separate ways. God said, "No," and my peace returned. He knew what was best for me.

What about when God is silent? My husband always says that the three most faithful words are "I don't know." God doesn't always answer the way we want Him to or think that He should.

My twelfth year was one of the worst of my life. I had just started my fourth school (in seventh grade) and my mom had moved us in with my godparents. After a few months of living there, my mom took off and we didn't hear from her for over a month. I seriously thought that she was dead in a ditch somewhere from driving drunk. (She happened to be in Texas with my aunt and uncle—a place she was planning on staying.) I enjoyed living with my godparents. I had a mom and a dad, two brothers, and lots of rules and regulations. Kids need boundaries. I definitely needed boundaries. I was heading in a bad way fast! My godmother was able to reign me in, and I loved living with that family. I was there for about five months when my godmother had asked if she could adopt me legally and I said "Yes!" I would have a real life with them. I was so excited until my mother called and I talked to her about the news.

All was well, until the next day in school. I was called to the principal's office because my "mother" was there to pick me up. I thought it was my godmother, but as I neared the office I could see it was my mom. She had driven up from Texas with my aunt and uncle to take me back. I begged and pleaded with them to take me to get my clothes and other stuff; they relented and took me back to the house. I ran in the house, shut and locked the door, and called my godmother, who, in turn, called the police. My mom, aunt, and uncle were all thrown off the property. It was a huge, messy fiasco. The sheriff talked to my mom and then came inside and talked to me and my godmother. I had to go with my mom. In the state of New Mexico, I was not old enough to make my own decisions, even though my mom had abandoned me. I cried—bent over, gut-groaning crying. I did not want to go, but I had no other choice. My godmother cried, the sheriff even cried. It was a horrible day. What I remember most was the drive home. I was crying out to God to let me go back to my godmother. I begged and pleaded with Him, but He never answered and He didn't send me back. That next year was another bad year, and another time I was molested by an older man that my mom had as a roommate.

I can't tell you why God didn't spare me from that pain. I can't tell you why He didn't let me live with my godmother in a good home. I don't know. This I do know: God is good and He sees the *whole story*. He saw my life from beginning to end and He knew where I would end up right now. I know that if I had not gone through the things I have gone through that I would not be the person I am today. Perhaps if I had lived a different life, I would not even be with Him. I would still be wandering.

Please listen! God is for you! He wants what's best for you and He can see the *whole* picture, while you are only able to see what's directly in front of you. He is watching out for your best interests and trying to keep you safe from harm when He tells you no. He knows where you will end up and if you will go down any different path than the one He has marked out for you. You have to learn to listen to His voice and obey His Word, even when He is silent. Be a good listener. His "no" is always for your good.

Chapter 28

Run Two Miles
with a Friend

A few weeks ago, Matt and I were running down on our favorite trail. It was a gorgeous, sixty-seven-degree morning, perfect running weather. Typically, on this trail, we run out two miles, back two miles, and Matt likes to do interval training on the two miles back, with a mixture of walking and running. I will run ahead and then run back to him so he can rest a little bit. He's not used to running four miles continuously.

On this particular day, we turned around at the two-mile marker and ran into an old friend that we hadn't seen on the trail in almost a year.

She has never stopped to run with us before, typically she'd be running in the opposite direction and we'd stop and exchange pleasantries. But, this day she asked if she could run with us. Now, this was an incredibly hard run for my husband. In addition to the distance, we were now running at a faster pace (because she's a seasoned runner). We found out a ton about her, her husband, her kids, what church she used to attend, what she was currently up to, and why she wasn't attending church. We were able to invite her to come and visit our church. We also found out a that a coach at her high school was also a coach at

Matt's high school. It was a pretty cool connection. We were able to talk to her for almost a full fifteen minutes. I was so proud of Matt. I knew how hard it was on him to run those extra 2 miles. He told me after he caught his breath that he just felt like the Lord wanted him to run and talk with her.

This is the God's heart. Run with your brothers and sister in Christ through life.

> "And whoever compels you to go one mile, go with him two" **Matthew 5:41.**

Go farther than you want or even think you are able. He wants you to walk through life with others. He uses us to refine each other.

> "As iron sharpens iron, so a man sharpens the countenance of his friend" **Proverbs 27:17. NKJV**

You were never meant to be a lone wolf Christian. You are meant to live, breath, and move in community with other believers. This is what the church is—it's not a building, it's the body of believers.

I'm not sure if you know this or recognize that the Bible was written to the believer in Christ, not the unbeliever. It was written to the church, the body of believers living together, trying to walk out the faith in the midst of a lost world. Jesus is coming back for His bride. I asked my husband one time that if someone professed their love for him and in the same breath declared how much they disliked me, how would that affect him? He replied that he would want nothing to do with that person. I am Matt's bride. This is a picture of Jesus and the church. It is a marriage relationship. The love we have for our brothers and sisters in Christ is a special kind of love that is supposed to look and act differently.

> "I give you a new commandment: that you should love one another. Just as I have loved you, so you too should love one another. By this shall all [men] know that you are My disciples, if you love one another [if you keep on showing love among yourselves]" John 13:34-35.

> "By this we know love, because He laid down His life for us. And we also ought to lay down our lives for the brethren" 1 John 3:16.

Remember others. The world without Christ will know us "by our love for *each other*"—each other being our brothers and sisters in Christ. The world will know we are different by the way we treat, serve, minister to, walk with, take care of our brethren in Christ. We are supposed to have a special relationship and fellowship with other believers.

Now, I am not saying that the church has done a great job at displaying this; some churches have done very poorly at loving one another. They will love and serve the world, but then chew up and spit out their brethren in Christ. These things should not be! But, you and I can change this. You and I can be the difference makers to this next generation of believers. It has to start somewhere. Why not with you? One person can make a difference.

If you have been hurt by a body of believers, choose *today* to forgive. Find a church where you can plug in and call home. Find a pastor that preaches the truth of God's Word and people who take their faith seriously, and then dig in! You start being a friend. You go visit a sick parishioner. You get involved in a Bible study or small group. If there's a need, You fill it. Don't expect someone else to do it, You can do it. Talk to your pastors and leaders and let them know what help ministries are needed and then you implement it. A good leader will walk with you until you can do it on your own, and then they will empower you to keep going.

You need accountability. You need encouragement. It's too easy to get off track. It's too easy to believe the lies of the enemy. It's too easy to get sucked into the traps of the world and the devil. You need your brothers and sisters in Christ as much as they need you. You are needed! You provide something that others can't. You have gifts that no one else has. You are unique and you are needed.

> "Not forsaking *or* neglecting to assemble together [as believers], as is the habit of some people, but admonishing (warning, urging, and encouraging) one another, and all the more faithfully as you see the day approaching" **Hebrews 10:25**.

I got caught in the trap of thinking that the church was supposed to meet all my needs; when truly God wanted to use me to meet other's needs in the Body. He wants to use you!

Going into the woods is not having "church." Sitting at home listening to preaching is not having "church." Going to the woods is great for solitary time. It's wonderful to listen to preaching on TV. However, church can only be experienced in the body of believers, where you come together with one mind and in one accord, worshiping and praising the Creator. Church is where the Spirit flows freely, where one prophecies and another sings songs, where still another has a gift of tongues, and yet another interprets. Church is where the pastor works with the prophet, the evangelist works with the teacher, all for the perfection of the saints of God. You cannot get any of this by yourself, or even with one friend. It takes a whole body of believers to run through life.

> "And he gave the apostles, the prophets, the evangelists, the shepherds and teachers, to equip the saints for the work of ministry, for building up the body of Christ, until we all attain to the unity of the faith and of the knowledge of the Son of God, to mature manhood, to the measure of the stature of the fullness of Christ, so that we may no longer be children, tossed to and fro by the waves and carried about by every wind of doctrine, by human cunning, by craftiness in deceitful schemes. Rather, speaking the truth in love, we are to grow up in every way into him who is the head, into Christ, from whom the whole body, joined and held together by every joint with which it is equipped, when each part is working properly, makes the body grow so that it builds itself up in love" **Ephesians 4:11-16.**

Paul is referring to the five-fold ministry: apostle, prophet, evangelist, pastor, and teacher. I have heard it said that this is the hand of God with each ministry being a finger. God revealed this to me: the apostle is the thumb—he is the foundation for which all others are built. The apostle is covered by the other fingers and the apostle covers the fingers. The prophet is the index finger—pointing and directing the right way path, exhorting and encouraging the Body to stay in the narrow Way. The pastor is the tallest center finger as the head of the local church. There is only one head and as Christ is the head of the whole Body, the pastor is the head of the local congregation.

My pastor in Texas always says that the only thing that has more than one head is the antichrist. That is wisdom.

The teacher is the ring finger, married to God's Word. If anyone claims to be a teacher and does not absolutely love and adore God's Word, then they are not a true teacher of God. Last, but certainly not least, is the pinky, the evangelist, who in appearance is the smallest, but has the largest voice. This is the John the Baptist, the voice of one crying in the wilderness, "Repent! Make the path straight for the return of Jesus! Repent and be baptized and you shall receive the gift of the Holy Ghost!" These five fingers work together in harmony. However, if a finger isn't working, it affects the whole hand.

My son was playing basketball a while back and he jammed his ring finger in an intense game of two on two. He had been lifting weights with his dad and me, but because his finger swelled up so much, he couldn't grip the bar. One finger affected his whole hand.

Like I said, you are needed in the church and you are of great value. Your absence affects the whole. Unfortunately, even in the church people will hurt you. But, you cannot let a hurt hinder you from doing your part in the body of Christ. Have you been church hurt? I have. I was a brand-new baby Christian and our youth group was going to an amusement park and needed some chaperones. Another lady and I decided we would go and have fun with the kiddos and be chaperones. On the way, we stopped at a house to pick up another friend. There, we were met by an elder Pentecostal woman, who was highly regarded in the church as a great woman of faith. I had heard of her and had respect for her.I was wearing a sundress with cap sleeves to expose my shoulders and the length hit just right at my knees. My friend was wearing a short-sleeved shirt with a long, denim skirt down to her ankles. This older woman looked me up and down, looked at my friend, and proceeded to say, "At least there is still some modesty among the young ladies today! Hmph!" And she walked away.

I was devastated. I could feel the tears welling up in my eyes. This woman didn't know anything about me. She didn't know my past hurts and abuses. She just proceeded to say exactly what she thought, and she didn't care if it hurt me or not. Yes, I was hurt.

I also had a woman tell me I was rebellious for wearing lip gloss in church. I could tell you stories of the pastoral abuse I've experienced, but I won't because it doesn't matter. The fact remains that God is still good and He is still the same. He didn't make those people do those things; they did them of their own free will. I'm still here. I'm still serving God and I'm still attending church most days of the week. If I had let those offenses keep me from church, I would not be the person I am today, and God would not be able to use me in the way He does to minister and run the race with others.

Let go of past hurts. Abandon your old thoughts about church. Get back in there! Someone needs you to run another two miles with them!

Now, sometimes you need a push from a brother or sister. I struggled to get back into my running after my son was born, and I was super slow. At this same time, Matt was probably at the height of his running career (this was back in 2000 while he was serving in the military and was forced to run). He was running close to seven-minute miles and he had to run at least three times a week, but he would make himself run four miles. We have always enjoyed doing things together, especially exercise.

About eight weeks after Gabriel was born, we flew to California to visit Matt's dad. The next morning, we got up early to go for a run and I was really, really dragging. My body was still healing from having a baby and I wasn't back to running on a regular basis. My beautiful husband would run beside me, with his hand on my lower back and push me as he was running. It sounds weird, but it makes a huge difference. I could keep up with him. It was like an extra force was behind me pushing me, lightening my load, and I could finish the run with him. We still do that for each other on our runs when one of us gets tired.

Yes! You have the Holy Spirit to give you that "push", but you could be that "push" for a brother or sister in Christ. Maybe you need that "push" right now in your life, and you can find it from a friend in Christ. The Lord knows right where you are and exactly what you need right now. Don't stop running! You still have to finish your race! Let someone push you. Let them help you when you are down, dragging, or just plain tired and worn out. Share your struggle with a trusted sister in Christ. Then, when you are back and running strong, you can be that "push" for another.

Do not listen to the lies of the enemy. You need the Body of Christ. You need someone to lift you up when you are down. You need the fellowship of the Saints and above all you are needed!

Chapter 29

The Power of a
New Pair of Shoes

Today I got a new pair of shoes. I love the smell and the feel of a new pair of my favorite shoes: Brooks. I couldn't wait to go for my first run in them! I got the chance two days later, and I was in heaven. I felt like I could run forever, like I was Forest running coast to coast with a seventies soundtrack playing in the background. It was like running on a cloud. I didn't want to stop.

I had forgotten what it was like getting a new pair of shoes. I like to really wear out my old ones, literally, until my feet hurt, until the soles of my shoes get holes in them, but that's not really good for my feet. Running in an old pair of shoes makes me feel humdrum. It's the same boring, old run and I'm going to wake up and do the same thing tomorrow—another boring, old run in my boring, old shoes, where my toes are rubbing together uncomfortably because the shoes are losing their form. Old shoes make me feel like I'm on repeat like that old Dunkin Donut commercial—the one where the donut guy gets up early and stays late, doing it again every day, "Time to make the donuts!" Just another humdrum day. However, a new pair of shoes reminds me how much I love running. It reminds me why I run and how running makes me feel good and relieves my stress. That is the power of a new day.

A new day can remind you why you serve and love Jesus and *today* is a new day. Today, you can be reminded of the joy you have in Christ. Today doesn't have to be a boring, humdrum, "just another day" day. It is a brand-new day. Today you can run from coast to coast. Today can remind you how good the Lord is. Today can remind you that you are saved and you can be reminded of the joy of your salvation. Let today be a *new day*.

When Matt was in the military, he had painful shin splits from running. Well, he thought they were from running, when actually they were from running with old shoes. As soon as we bought him a new pair of good running shoes, it completely changed his outlook on running. He began to like running because he wasn't in pain anymore. He thought, *I can run today!* It gave him a new outlook on running.

A new day will do that for you. A new day lets you know the past and the pain was yesterday and today is a new day. Today you can run pain free. A new day brings new memories and new joys. Forget about the pain from yesterday; today you have new shoes and you can run!

If you are reading this right now, you woke up this morning. There is still breath in your lungs. You have been given another chance, another do-over. I remember what it felt like when I woke up after I overdosed. I was overjoyed that I was still alive. Yes, I still had struggles in front of me, but I was alive. You are still here and you are still alive. You have been given the gift of a new day. What will you do with it? Will you run, or will you retreat?

My husband is funny. He will never run two days in a row! His excuse is, "I ran yesterday." Okay...? That was yesterday. It's today. I don't care that you ran yesterday. Today you have new shoes. Today is the present. Today is a brand-new day. Today you have to run. It doesn't matter that you ran yesterday. Run today. Period.

I think a lot of people have this same mentality. I did the dishes *yesterday*. I did the laundry *yesterday*. I went to work *yesterday*. I made dinner *yesterday*.

Well, that's great; but those things need to be done *today*. Today is the present. We are living in "today," not the yesterdays of the world, and you woke up today and are still alive!

"You shall therefore keep His statutes and His commandments which I command you today, that it may go well with you and with your children after you, and that you may prolong *your* days in the land which the LORD your God is giving you for all time" **Deuteronomy 4:40**

"And Moses called all Israel, and said to them: 'Hear, O Israel, the statutes and judgments which I speak in your hearing today, that you may learn them and be careful to observe them'" **Deuteronomy 5:1.**

"The LORD did not make this covenant with our fathers, but with us, those who *are* here today, all of us who *are* alive" **Deuteronomy 5:3.**

"And these words which I command you today shall be in your heart" **Deuteronomy 6:6.**

God is a *today* God, right now, ever present. He does not live in the past, He lives *today*. He moves *today*. He acts *today*. We are not promised tomorrow; therefore, we are told to not even worry about it.

"Therefore do not worry about tomorrow, for tomorrow will worry about its own things. Sufficient for the day *is* its own trouble" **Matthew 6:34.**

Are we not told, "Give us *this day* our daily bread?" You need to live with the mindset of this day.

Today, what can I do for the Lord? Today, where can I go for Him? What can He change in me today? How can I help someone today? Today I have work to do for Him. Today I have a race to run.

It doesn't matter what you did yesterday. Yesterday is gone and today is a brand-new day! You have new shoes!

Do you need healing? Today go and get your healing. Lay in the Master's arms and feel His arms wrap around you and fill that void. Do you need deliverance? Today cast down that stronghold and hold fast to His unchanging Word. Do you need forgiveness? Today repent and ask and He will cast your sins as far as the east is from the west. Have you been living with guilt and shame? Today let Him wash you clean.

Today he wants to heal you. Today he wants to deliver you. Today he wants to forgive you. Today he wants to restore you. Today he wants to make you a new vessel. Today he wants to come and love you.

He wants to meet your needs today.

Maybe you're okay with your past, but you worry too much about the future. I think it's so easy to get up in the mindset of "I'll do this when...." or "I'll be happy when...." Well, what if the "when" never happens?

I overdosed while snorting speed when I was seventeen. It was a huge turning point in my life. I almost died, if not for the grace of a God I didn't know, serve, or love, but in the midst of my suffering I called out to Him. Nobody at the party would take me to the ER, so I lay down on the floor to die, but in a final ditch effort, I called out to the Lord to save me because I didn't want to go to hell. Somehow, I knew that if I died at that time I was not destined for heaven. I didn't know anything about heaven, but I knew hell was not a place I wanted to be a part of.

I felt a hand come into my chest and He kept my heart beating all night, when it should have stopped. I would still be six more years until I finally surrendered to Him and was born again of His Spirit.

After I was born again, I began praying:

"Lord, I will do whatever you want me to do *after* you heal me."

The overdose left me with circulation problems and heart rhythm problems. I was up at the altar every single time asking for healing, so I could be used. After a couple of years of waiting to be healed before I did anything, the Lord spoke to me:

"I am enough for you. Do not worry about your healing. Will you still serve Me, even if you never get healed?"

Well, the "when" never came and here I am twenty years later, still not healed of those problems, but fully immersed in serving and being used of God. (Although, I have been healed in so many other areas.) He has healed my heart and my emotions, and most definitely my soul.

Do I still hope and believe to receive a physical healing? You betcha! But, I would never be where I am in life if I had kept adhering to that ultimatum. I would still be in the same place, with the same thoughts, crying those same tears, waiting for the "when." You cannot live for tomorrow. You cannot wait to be used tomorrow. You have to stop waiting for the "when."

Have you ever had the thought that you would make amends

with someone at a later date? What if that day never comes? What if they die, or for that matter, you die? How long will you wait to forgive? How long will you wait to say, "I love you"? Time doesn't always make things better, sometimes it makes people more bitter. Time can increase the chasm that is between you and another.

I know a person that had to wait until the day his mother died to hear her say, "I love you." Seriously, the only time in his whole life that his mom told him that she loved him was on her death bed?! How sad is that?

What are you waiting for? Death comes for us all and at a time when we don't always expect it. Make the most of this day!

Choose this day to be happy! Choose this day to live! Choose this day, choose life and joy! Choose this day to go forth!

Do not wait until tomorrow. Today is the day of salvation and you've just been given a new pair of running shoes! What are you waiting for? Get out there and hit the pavement!

Chapter 30

Ears to Hear

I have a few cardinal rules I follow for running outside. One is that I always run against traffic. This way you can see the cars coming at you. I know this is the standard rule for walking, too, but I learned this the hard way.

Some lady on her phone was coming up the hill behind me and she dropped it, then swerved all the way on the shoulder, missing me by only about a foot. She never even noticed me. The reason I knew it was a phone that dropped was because I saw her bending down to pick it up as she passed me by and then put it back to her ear. I even tried yelling, but she never noticed. After that incident, I run facing traffic. The second rule, which most everyone breaks, is you should never run outside with headphones. Women running alone especially need to be able to hear their surroundings. You need to be aware of what is going on around you, traffic, sirens, other people, etc. When I was younger, I would run with headphones (I still do at the gym occasionally) until I was cautioned by several people that I needed to be able to hear everything and stay alert.

The other day, I was out on my run through the neighborhood. I have a path that I run, and there's a right turn that switches directly into a left turn. The oncoming cars are supposed to stop at the top of the hill before turning right, but no one ever stops, or even slows down for that matter. I was coming around the corner and I would normally cut the corner short, but I heard a car coming up the hill and so I got all the way to the right-hand side. If I had not been able to hear the car, I would have been hit. He didn't slow down and I would have been exactly in the right place at the wrong time. I was seriously praising God that I heard that car and was able to move in time to not be hit.

> Do you have ears to hear what the Spirit is saying in these last days, or are you walking around with your headphones on, completely oblivious to your surroundings? Jesus cried out time and time again: "If anyone has ears to hear, let him hear" **Mark 7:16.**

Do you have ears to hear? Or are you dull of hearing? Spiritual things can only be discerned spiritually.

> "But the natural man does not receive the things of the Spirit of God, for they are foolishness to him; nor can he know them, because they are spiritually discerned" **1 Corinthians 2:14.**

Are your ears open and are you ready to receive what the Spirit is saying? He is speaking. He speaks to us through His Word and by His Spirit, but also through supernatural means like visions and dreams (if you pay attention).

> "Now the Spirit expressly says that in latter times some will depart from the faith, giving heed to deceiving spirits and doctrines of demons, speaking lies in hypocrisy, having their own conscience

seared with a hot iron, forbidding to marry, and commanding to abstain from foods which God created to be received with thanksgiving by those who believe and know the truth" 1 Timothy 4:1-3.

This Word is for us now. It is referring to the great apostasy, a falling away from the faith concerning a large portion of the church because of "deceiving spirits and doctrines of demons." Are your headphones off? Are you listening?

My ministry gift is that of a prophet. I struggled with my calling for a long time; I didn't want it. It is a heavy burden to carry. But I wanted to honor God with my life and I surrendered my will. I was not going to throw God's gift back in His face. Instead I said, "Here I am God, send me." So, He did. His will. His way. I am just His vessel. I must speak what He tells me to speak. I must share what He tells me to share. He has given me Word for this next upcoming season and it concerns "deceiving spirits."

"If anyone teaches otherwise and does not consent to wholesome words, even the words of our Lord Jesus Christ, and to the doctrine which accords with godliness, he is proud, knowing nothing, but is obsessed with disputes and arguments over words, from which come envy, strife, reviling, evil suspicions, useless wranglings of men of corrupt minds and destitute of the truth, who suppose that godliness is a means of gain. From such withdraw yourself" 1 Timothy 6:3-5.

Read 2 Timothy 3; 4:1–5 and Exo 7:11–12 .as a reference. The Lord spoke this word to me about this next season:

"A counterfeit move of the Spirit has infiltrated My people. They seek after a sign and the only sign that will be given is of Jonahrepent or perish. My people do not know Me, they only know their own ways. A strong delusion is coming so that those who continually refuse and reject My ways will not be able to believe the truth. I have given them space to repent. The time is coming when even the very elect will be deceived. You cannot continue to reject Me and My ways and think that I will look the other way. The time is coming. Crystal, you must warn my people. My heart is broken. I am grieved with this generation. You are my watchman. Tell my people to repent or they will suffer My wrath. They will perish. There is a counterfeit gospela counterfeit spirit. It wants its own way. It seeks its own pleasure. It is greedy and full of lusts. It is full of deceit. My gospel produces righteousness. My gospel produces holiness and humility. My pastors will rise to the top. I will exalt their voices. My pastors will preach righteousness. Deception is widespread. Stay in My Word and at My feet. Stay in My Word. Be grounded and level."

There are things coming in the next few years that will greatly affect America, in fact the American foundation has been eroded and we are going to fall as a nation. The face of America is going to change.

We are in the last days. Did you realize that we are in the book of Revelation right now? The first book I ever read in the Bible was Revelation. Sure, most people would start with something a little lighter, perhaps Mark or John, but not me.

The year before I overdosed, I saw the movie *The Seventh Sign*, and it got me curious. So, I found a Bible and I read Revelation for myself. I did not understand it at that time, but I did understand that Jesus was real and He was coming back, and I knew I wasn't ready. It was the reason I was able to call out to

God while I lay on the floor dying of an overdose. Yes, the book of Revelation can reveal Jesus to people. Actually, it is my favorite book of the Bible because it is the culmination of all things. It is the book that reveals who Jesus is *right now*—King of kings and Lord of lords, high and lifted up! I have been a student of the Book of Revelation for over twenty years. I just love it. It is full of Jesus's words to the church and His view of what has been going on, good and bad, with His church.

Guess what? Jesus is speaking to us today: "He who has an ear, let him hear what the Spirit says to the churches" **Revelation 2:7.**

> "He who has an ear, let him hear what the Spirit says to the churches" **Revelation 2:11.**

> "He who has an ear, let him hear what the Spirit says to the churches" **Revelation 2:17.**

> "He who has an ear, let him hear what the Spirit says to the churches" **Revelation 2:29.**

> "He who has an ear, let him hear what the Spirit says to the churches" **Revelation 3:6.**

> "He who has an ear, let him hear what the Spirit says to the churches" **Revelation 3:13.**

> "He who has an ear, let him hear what the Spirit says to the churches" **Revelation 3:22.**

Out of the seven churches in Revelation, five receive severe condemnation and were told to repent. This same Word is for today. This is the call for America: Repent! The American church is in a bad, bad state, far past a lukewarm state of trouble.

Be careful who you are listening to. There are a lot of false prophets out there, prophesying things to please people and "tickle" their ears.

> "For false christs and false prophets will rise and show great signs and wonders to deceive, if possible, even the elect" **Matthew 24:24.**

> "But there were also false prophets among the people, even as there will be false teachers among you, who will secretly bring in destructive heresies, even denying the Lord who bought them, and bring on themselves swift destruction" **2 Peter 2:1.**

There is a false gospel of love and grace. Love is being preached, but it's not the love of God. It's a worldly love, full of lust and self-love. It's humanistic in nature—loving and exalting the creation above the Creator—and its end is destruction. The false love gospel seeks to elevate human kind. False love cares more for man's comfort than for his soul. False love seeks to please men and receive gratitude, it's allegiances are misplaced.

Oswald Chambers in *My Utmost for His Highest* said this: "*The chief motivation behind Paul's service was not love for others, but love for His Lord. If our devotion is to the cause of humanity, we will be quickly defeated and broken-hearted, since we will often be confronted with a great deal of ingratitude from other people. But, if we are motivated by our love for God, no amount of ingratitude will be able to hinder us from serving one another.*"

However, God's love, the agape love that flows from a heart that is entirely captivated by Jesus is different:

> "Love suffers long and is kind; love does not envy; *love does not parade itself,* is not puffed up; does not behave rudely, does not seek its own, is not provoked, thinks no evil; *does not rejoice in iniquity, but rejoices in the truth;* bears all things, believes all things, hopes all things, endures all things"
> **1 Corinthians 13:4-7.**

Grace is being preached, but it's not God's grace. It's not the grace that leads to transformation and denying oneself. It is not the grace that teaches us to be different and to repent and crucify the flesh. It is not *charis* being preached, and grace is never, never, ever obscene.

> "For the grace of God that brings salvation has appeared to all men, teaching us that, denying ungodliness and worldly lusts, we should live soberly, righteously, and godly in the present age, looking for the blessed hope and glorious appearing of our great God and Savior Jesus Christ, who gave Himself for us, that He might redeem us from every lawless deed and purify for Himself His own special people, zealous for good works" **Titus 2:11-14.**

Take off your headphones and hear what the Spirit is saying. Drown out every noise that is not of God or from God, turn off the TV, get off the computer, and get into your word and in prayer. Find a church that is preaching the entire word and counsel of God. He is speaking to you. The time is short. Will you listen?

Do you have ears to hear? The Lord has recently spoken to me saying, "Batten down the hatches." Church, we need to be prepared for a storm that is barreling down on us. You cannot *get ready*, you need to *be ready*. God has to do something to wake up His church to repentance; otherwise, we will be lost with the world. He does not want us to fear, but only trust and believe. He always takes care of His own. Even Shadrach, Meshach, and Abednigo had to go through the fire, but He got in there with them. Yes, going through is always God's way.

> "When you pass through the waters, I will be with you; And through the rivers, they shall not overflow you. When you walk through the fire, you shall not be burned, Nor shall the flame scorch you" **Isaiah 43:2.**

You must have your spiritual ears open while you are running your race, so you do not come around a blind corner and get squashed! Be ready! Go out prepared. Take off your headphones that are pumping in the world's message and tune in to the Holy Spirit.

Chapter 31

Run, Saint, Run!

Have I persuaded you to start running yet? My hope is that not only will you hit the track, but you will begin to run the race set before you, and you'll run it with everything in you. It's time to stop making excuses. Time is short.

"Besides this you know what [a critical] hour this is, how it is high time now for you to wake up out of your sleep (rouse to reality). For salvation (final deliverance) is nearer to us now than when we first believed (adhered to, trusted in, and relied on Christ, the Messiah). The night is far gone and the day is almost here. Let us then drop (fling away) the works *and* deeds of darkness and put on the [full] armor of light. Let us live and conduct ourselves honorably *and* becomingly as in the [open light of] day, not in reveling (carousing) and drunkenness, not in immorality and debauchery (sensuality and licentiousness), not in quarreling and jealousy. But clothe yourself with the Lord Jesus Christ (the Messiah), and make no provision for [indulging] the flesh [put a stop to thinking about the evil cravings of your physical nature] to [gratify its] desires (lusts)" **Romans 13:11-14.**

I am for you! God is for you! You *can* run this race.

"Have you not known? Have you not heard? The everlasting God, the Lord, the Creator of the ends of the earth, does not faint or grow weary; there is no searching of His understanding. He gives power to the faint *and* weary, and to him who has no might He increases strength [causing it to multiply and making it to abound]. Even youths shall faint and be weary, and [selected] young men shall feebly stumble *and* fall exhausted; But those who wait for the Lord [who expect, look for, and hope in Him] shall change *and* renew their strength *and* power; they shall lift their wings *and* mount up [close to God] as eagles [mount up to the sun]; they shall run and not be weary, they shall walk and not faint *or* become tired" **Isaiah 40:28-31.**

Did you read that? Do you hear Him? You will run and not grow weary—if you wait on the Lord. What does it mean to "wait?" Some see waiting as waiting to be seen by a doctor. Sitting, doing nothing, and waiting for something to happen, either for good or bad, but just waiting. This is not the waiting God wants from us.

I like to picture waiting like a medieval "lady in waiting," or a waitress at a five-star restaurant. I am always in my Lord's presence. Sometimes sitting at His feet, sometimes standing at the ready, I wait on Him. I wait for His orders, but I still have other tables to wait on. I still have a job to do while I am waiting on Him. I wait for His requests, "Would you like more water? Can I get you more bread? Would you like a clean fork?" I wait for His answer. I wait on my other tables. I wait for His healing. I wait to be delivered. I wait to be restored, yet at the same time I am running my race, doing the things that I know am suppose to be doing. I wait on Him, ready to go, ready to do and always, always expecting, trusting and believing that He knows what is best, and He has perfect timing. God's timing is always perfect. He is a right-on-time God. Often, when we are running we can get ahead of His timing, leave Him in the dust and find ourselves lost. Waiting always has to do with God's timing. He is never late and never early. He is the Lord of time and has a perfect time for your ministry.

Are you getting dizzy and tired of waiting? There is always a reason God has you in a holding pattern. When Gabriel was about four months old, we flew to California to visit my father-in-law. We lived in a small town in Texas called Killeen, and so for the return flight we had a flight into Dallas and then had to take a smaller plane. We found out there was a bad storm, and so we were held in a circling pattern over Killeen for literally and hour. The storm was so bad they redirected us back to Dallas and we had to take a flight out the next day. There is a reason God has you in a waiting season. You never know what He is saving you from by keeping you waiting. In the waiting, He is also working on your character and developing your trust in Him.

This waiting is active, not passive. Waiting expects that He is going to move, He is going to heal, He is going to deliver. Having an expectation that God is working on your behalf requires faith. You will not run well without faith. Everything with the Lord is activated by your faith in Him, even grace is activated by faith. "For by grace are you saved, through faith." Ephesians 2: 8. Faith is required to move those proverbial mountains. It is required to run your race; otherwise, you will run aimlessly. Faith is not a "hope-so-hope," but rather a "know-so-hope." Faith is an as-surance that God will see you through your battles and that He will gain you the victory. Yet, you still have to wait on the Lord's time! Do what He asks of you and somewhere in this process of waiting, He will meet your needs and you will run your race with assurance.

Running your race well is predicated on you waiting on the Lord's timing and obeying the Word of God and the Holy Spirit.

I have run in a lot of different areas. One place in California is super windy. It's beautiful and sunny, but windy nonetheless. Sometimes on my run, the wind is at my back pushing me along and my run is effortless. I can run faster and longer. But that same run, ran against the wind, is like running uphill in the sand wearing cement shoes carrying a heavy pack on my back. It's tough and exhausting. This is the battle. You are called to crucify the flesh and live in agreement with the Holy Spirit; letting Him lead and guide you in His path. When you are in agreement with the Spirit, it is like running with the wind at your back. Life is peaceful and smooth. Even walking through that valley of the shadow of death you are comforted when the Spirit is leading you.

Yet, run in opposition to the Spirit and you grow tired and weary. Since the flesh is contrary to the Spirit, you find yourself battling the Spirit, running against the wind.

"For as many as are led by the Spirit of God, these are sons of God" **Romans 8:14.**

We are only considered sons and daughters of the most High if we are *led* by Him; otherwise we are still illegitimate children. I remember the first time I found out what the word "bastard" meant—a child with no father. I was young and went around telling people that I was a bastard. Seriously. Kids are naïve and I didn't understand the negative connotations behind that word.

It's an ugly word and I don't like it. I am no longer illegitimate, I am a daughter of God. I am led by the Spirit of God, being brought into unity with Him.

You are not like everyone else; therefore, you cannot do what everyone else does. I learned this lesson at an early age. *"If everyone jumped off the Empire State Building, would you?"* I was asked that question a lot as a child, always after I misbehaved or was tempted to. So, would you?

My mom was quite the hippy, which means I grew up around hippies, and in a "hippy atmosphere"–i.e. around a lot of nudity. I remember at the age of four, we used to go to a local waterfall to play and all the adults would go naked. I can still remember feeling awkward about being naked, but the longer I was around it, the less awkward it became.

There came a time that my mom was having a party and as the night progressed and the drinking and drugs escalated, the clothes started coming off. By this time, I was close to six years old. I decided that I should take off my shirt along with everyone else. There was one lady at the party who still had her shirt on and she grabbed me, took me to my room, shut the door, and told me to put on my shirt and stay in my room. She told me that I was a young lady and that young ladies do not do take off their shirt no matter what everyone else is doing. She made an impression on me.

To run this race, you are going have to be different than the crowd. Even in some Christian circles, you are going to have to be different. In the Christian world, there is still a lot of pressure to do what everyone else is doing and the crowd is a courage killer. Do you know the book *The Prayer of Jabez*? Or how about *A Purpose Driven Life*? These books are bestsellers and I remember hearing all the time, "You haven't read it yet? Everyone is doing it! You have to read it, too!" Sound familiar? Well, I read them, and I loved both books, but there is huge pressure to conform, even in Christiandom. While these books are engaging and have a strong message and benefits, they are not the Bible. There is wisdom in reading good Christian books, but you are only responsible before God for reading the Bible, not any other book, even this one. Books contain the author's view point. Even backed up with facts, or Scripture; this book is still based on my experiences. You must seek discernment with what you allow to enter your mind. Yes, even in Christian circles! I pray that sharing a part of my story will benefit and help you to run your race! But, if it doesn't line up with God's Word, no matter how popular it is, then you need to cast it aside.

A while ago, some company came out with these new running shoes that had rubber toe slots for each toe. I thought those shoes looked stupid and, apparently, they ended up causing problems with some people's feet. I haven't seen a pair in a while. But they were created because the new big thing was running on your toes.

Now, I tried these shoes because everyone was doing it, but they didn't really work for me. They created unnecessary pain when running. My old shoes were great! Plus, I had already purchased those flashy Nikes and learned my lesson there.

There is a sense of having good form when it comes to your feet placement. I have found for myself that the best form is landing on the middle of my foot and rounding up to my toes as I take each new stride. This seems to put less pressure on my knees and shins, rendering a satisfying, pain-free run. So, why would I try silly-looking rubber toe shoes? Why? Well, everyone was doing it and I got curious. I decided to conform, follow the crowd.

You are unique. You are going to run your race differently

than your Christian friends. You look different. You have a different calling and different gifts. You even run differently than others because you have a different stride. Don't get caught up in the comparison game. Comparison not only steals your joy, but it can cause bitterness and resentment. I like the ballerina analogy. You see the beautiful ballet dance, but you cannot see the ballerina's mangled toes. You have no idea how hard someone else has worked to get where they are in their faith. You don't see how long they have prayed and waited. You do not know the pain and suffering they have gone through, nor can you see their battle scars. Are you even willing to do what is takes to get where they are in the faith? Run *your* race. Stay in *your* lane.

Dear Saint, I plead with you to run this race set before you. Run with God. Run with the wind at your back. Run with the Spirit leading you, guiding you, and prompting you. Obey the Spirit. Run differently. Don't go the way of the crowd. Put the Word of God into your heart. Do these things and you shall never fail!

You have a race to run.

Will you run the race set before you?

Epilogue

My beloved yellow lab passed away earlier this year. He was getting old, his kidneys were failing, and his hips consistently gave out. We had to put him down. This might have been the hardest thing I've ever had to do. My son came in the vet's room with me on that day. Earlier, we took Ranger through the McDonald's drive-through and bought him two cheeseburgers, a small fry, and an ice cream cone. Ranger had not been eating much over the last few months, but he scarfed his last meal down. My son held Ranger's head in his lap and pet him, lovingly telling him what a good dog he had been, and expressing his love for him. My son had this dog his whole young life. It was heartbreaking. Ranger's passing left a huge silence in our home, and I literally could not stop crying. A couple of weeks had passed, and I decided I should pick up the rest of his doggy poop out of the backyard. My husband came home to me hysterically sobbing—over poop. "What's the matter honey?" Matt asked. "I cannot stop crying," I replied. And then the Lord spoke something very profound to me. I had never mourned anything I had been through. My life was a series of statements with the attitude, "Just get over it, kid, and move on! Life is not fair!" and now it was all coming out. Years of stuffing things down. Years of emotional hurts that I had never allowed to affect me. It was all coming out. The Lord gave me permission to mourn my life. I mourned for the innocence lost from my childhood. Healing came through the death of a big, hairy, crazy, lovable, yellow dog.

If you are hurting, sit still in the presence of the Lord. Let Him heal you wholly. Don't get stuck there, but do not move on too quickly. He can and will heal all pains, emotional and physical, if you let Him. Give all your hurt and pain to Him. He cares for you and He has a healing for you. He has a plan to make you whole. His healing is perfect. There is nothing He cannot heal and make whole, if you let Him. And above all, keep running your race.

> "But none of these things move me; nor do I count my life dear to myself, so that I may finish my race with joy, and the ministry which I received from the Lord Jesus, to testify to the gospel of the grace of God"
> **Acts 20:24. NKJV**